Crypto Investment for Beginners: A Step-by-Step Guide to Understanding and Profiting from the Cryptocurrency Market 4

About the Author 4

Motivation 5

Summary 6

Chapter 1: Introduction to Cryptocurrency Investing 8

1.0 Introduction 8

    1.1.2 Benefits of Crypto Investing 16

    1.3 Benefits and Risks of Crypto Investing 27

Chapter 2: Getting Started with Cryptocurrency Investments 39

2.0 Introduction 39

    2.1 Understanding the Technology 46
        2.1.1 Evaluating the Underlying Technology 47

    2.3 Use Case and Adoption 58
        2.3.1 Analyse the real-world use case and adoption potential of a cryptocurrency 59
        2.3.2 Look for partnerships, collaborations, and integrations with established companies or industries 61
        2.4.1 Impact of Regulations 64
        2.4.2 Assessing the Impact of Regulations on Growth and Adoption 66

    2.5 Investment Risks 68

    2.6 Technical Analysis 74
        2.6.1 Learn how to analyse price charts, patterns, and indicators to predict future price movements 74
        2.6.4 Evaluating Fundamental Factors 81

    2.8 Sentiment Analysis 88
        2.8.1 Learn sentiment analysis techniques to determine the overall market sentiment about a particular cryptocurrency 91
        2.8.2 Monitor social media platforms, online forums, and news articles to understand the sentiment of investors and the public 93

Chapter 3: Fundamental Concepts of Crypto Investment 109

3.0 Introduction 109

3.3 Security and Wallet Management 113

Chapter 4: Strategies for Successful Crypto Investments 118

4.0 Introduction 118

Chapter 5: Tools and Resources for Crypto Investors 128

5.0 Introduction 128

5.4 Tax Reporting Tools 133

Chapter 6: Overcoming Challenges in Crypto Investing 141

6.0 Introduction 141

Chapter 7: Real-Life Examples and Case Studies 149

7.0 Introduction 149

Chapter 8: Conclusion and Next Steps 156

8.0 Introduction 156

8.1 Recap of Key Points 158

Reference 161

Crypto Investment for Beginners: A Step-by-Step Guide to Understanding and Profiting from the Cryptocurrency Market

By Coleman Onwuzurike

About the Author

The author of the publication titled "Crypto Investment for Beginners" is
a dedicated trader who possesses expertise in the fields of cryptocurrency trading as well as stock

markets.

With
a proven history of effectively managing investments for clients and consistently generating weekly profits, the author also serves as a respected educator and mentor for individuals seeking to expand their knowledge of cryptocurrency.

With a profound comprehension of the cryptocurrency market and a dedication to facilitating the success of others, the author provides valuable insights and expertise in this book.

Motivation

The author's goal in writing "Crypto Investing for Beginners" is to educate and assist individuals who are new to the field. This book provides ample information on cryptocurrency investing.
As cryptocurrencies gain more and more widespread acceptance, the
author acknowledges the importance of having an all-encompassing guide that simplifies investing in them and offers practical ways to profit from the market. It's a great way to get people on board with this exciting and

growing industry.' The author, who has become entrepreneur and trainer, says it gives her inspiration to keep pushing forward.

Summary

In Chapter 1, readers are introduced to the fundamentals of cryptocurrency investing. The lesson they will be exposed to is how crypto money works, why it pays to invest in these cryptocurrencies, and
the advantages and disadvantages of doing so.

Chapter 2 guides readers through the process of getting started with cryptocurrency investments. It covers everything from opening up a digital wallet to choosing the right cryptocurrencies to invest, and even breaking down and analysing market trends.

Chapter 3 delves into the fundamental concepts of crypto investment. The reader will be provided with a thorough understanding of blockchain technology, cryptocurrency mining, proof-of-stake, and wallet management.

In Chapter 4, readers will discover strategies for successful crypto
investments. The topics covered will include understanding

long-term and short-term investing, balancing dollar costs with portfolio diversification, as well as discovering promising projects and ICOs.

Chapter 5 provides readers with a comprehensive list of tools and resources for crypto investors. It includes crypto exchanges and trading platforms, cryptocurrency news and analysis sites, and the monitoring of crypto market data.

Chapter 6 addresses the challenges that crypto investors may face. Readers will learn how to deal with volatility and market corrections, avoid scams and fraudulent projects, and navigate taxation and legal considerations.

Chapter 7 presents real-life examples and case studies of successful crypto investors, as well as lessons learned from failed investments.

In Chapter 8, readers will find a conclusion and next steps. This chapter summarizes the book and underscores that it is crucial to establish a comprehensive investment strategy for crypto assets, while also staying current with market developments.

With its comprehensive content and step-by-step approach, Crypto Investment for Beginners is the ultimate guide for those who are new to the cryptocurrency market and want to profit from their investments."

Chapter 1: Introduction to Cryptocurrency Investing

1.0 Introduction

In recent times, blockchain technology has become a decentralized network that is used to exchange digital currency on the internet. This chapter will delve into the intricacies of what constitutes cryptocurrency, the reasons behind investors' interest in investing in them, and the potential risks associated with this investment.

Cryptocurrency is becoming a revolutionary new currency that has caught the attention of people, businesses, and investors globally. It operates on a decentralized network called blockchain, which ensures transparency, security, and immutability. The purpose of this chapter is to provide a thorough overview of cryptocurrency investing, explaining its history, key concepts, and the reasons behind its growing popularity.

Cryptocurrency is a digital or virtual form of currency that utilizes cryptographic technology for secure financial transactions. Unlike traditional fiat currencies issued by governments, cryptocurrencies are decentralized and operate on a peer-to-peer network. This decentralization eliminates the need for intermediaries, such as banks, to conduct transactions. The most well-known cryptocurrency is Bitcoin, which was introduced in 2009 by an anonymous person or group known as Satoshi Nakamoto.

Investing in cryptocurrencies offers several advantages that have attracted a growing number of individuals and institutions. One of the primary advantages is the potential for high returns. Cryptocurrencies have experienced significant price appreciation over the years, resulting in substantial profits for early adopters and investors. By being decentralized, cryptocurrencies offer users more control over their financial activities and assets, providing them with greater autonomy. This is not the case for traditional financial systems.

Moreover, cryptocurrency investments can enhance the diversification of investment portfolios. By having a low correlation between cryptocurrencies and traditional asset classes like stocks and bonds, they can be considered as an attractive option for diversified portfolios. This diversification can help mitigate overall investment risk and potentially enhance returns. The risks associated with cryptocurrency investment are significant, despite the potential benefits. One of the primary risks is the volatility of cryptocurrency prices. Despite this, the value of cryptocurrencies can fluctuate rapidly over short periods, leading to significant gains or losses for investors. This volatility is influenced by factors such as market demand, regulatory developments, and investor sentiment.

Another risk is the potential for fraudulent activities and security breaches. The digital nature of cryptocurrencies makes them susceptible to hacking attempts and scams. Investors must take precautions to secure their digital wallets and choose reputable cryptocurrency exchanges for trading. Additionally, regulatory uncertainty poses a risk to cryptocurrency investing. Governments around the world are still developing regulations to govern cryptocurrencies, which can affect their acceptance and legality. Changes in regulations can impact investor sentiment and the overall cryptocurrency market.

Cryptocurrency investing has gained significant attention and popularity in recent years. Those seeking alternative investment options due to its decentralized nature, potential for high returns, and diversification benefits have found value in this asset class. However, it is important for investors to be aware of the risks associated with investing in cryptocurrencies, including price volatility, security risks and regulatory uncertainty. By understanding these factors, individuals can make informed investment decisions and navigate the dynamic world of cryptocurrency investing.

1.1 What is Cryptocurrency?

In this section we will look at the basic concepts of cryptocurrency. We examine the history of cryptocurrency, its technology, and how it deviates from conventional forms of money.

Cryptocurrency was introduced by Bitcoin in 2009 by an unknown person or group named Satoshi Nakamoto.Numerous other digital currencies have been int roduced, each with its own distinct characteristics and objectives. The decentralized nature of cryptocurrencies means that they are not controlled by a central authority such as a government or financial institution. Instead, transactions are verified and recorded on a distributed ledger called a blockchain.

To further explain the technology behind cryptocurrency, we can use the example of Bitcoin. Bitcoin runs on a decentralized network of computers called nodes. These nodes work together to validate and record transactions on the blockchain. Each transaction is encrypted and linked to the previous transaction, creating a chain of blocks. This ensures the security and immutability of the transaction history.

Besides, digital currencies employ cryptographic methods to safeguard transactions and regulate the production of new units. The Mining is the term used to describe the process of verifying transactions by solving complex mathematical problems and uploading them to the blockchain. Miners are rewarded with newly created cryptocurrency units as an incentive for their computational work.

One of the key advantages of cryptocurrency is its potential for increased financial inclusivity. Traditional financial systems often have barriers to entry, such as high transaction fees, limited access to banking services, and lengthy transaction settlement times. Cryptocurrencies, on the other hand, can provide individuals in underserved regions with access to financial services without the need for a traditional bank account. This can empower individuals and businesses by enabling faster, cheaper, and more secure cross-border transactions.

Additionally, cryptocurrencies provide privacy and anonymity that is not present in traditional financial systems. While transactions on the blockchain are transparent and can be viewed by anyone, the identities of the parties involved are often pseudonymous. Individuals can gain greater control over their financial transactions and privacy.

The unauthorized use of digital currencies has led to concerns about potential risks, such as money laundering and illegal transactions. The decentralized and borderless nature of cryptocurrencies can make it more challenging for authorities to track and regulate these activities. Therefore, there are demands for more stringent regulatory monitoring to mitigate these
concerns and maintain the advantages of cryptocurrencies.

To illustrate the impact of cryptocurrencies, let's consider the case study of Venezuela. The country has been facing severe economic challenges, including hyperinflation and a lack of access to traditional banking services. The case study of Venezuela exemplifies the impact of cryptocurrencies. Venezuelans can now rely on Bitcoin to protect their assets from the depreciation of their local currency, thanks to the system's ability to bypass traditional financial systems.

Apart from Bitcoin, there are several other digital currencies that have distinct functions and applications. Ethereum, for example, introduced the concept of smart contracts, which are self-executing contracts with the terms of the agreement directly written into lines of code. By using these smart contracts, it enables the automation and decentralization of processes like crowdfunding and supply chain management.

Ultimately, cryptocurrencies are virtual currency forms that work on the blockchain-based decentralized network. They offer increased financial inclusivity, privacy, and potential for innovation through technologies like smart contracts. Nonetheless, they also involve problems related to regulatory control and criminal activities.

To fully grasp the basics of cryptocurrency, it is essential for both individuals and businesses to understand the underlying concepts and potential benefits associated with digital currencies.

1.1.1 Statistics and Data

- As of September 2021, there are over 11,000 cryptocurrencies listed on various exchanges

worldwide, with a total market capitalization exceeding $2 trillion.
- Bitcoin, the first and most well-known cryptocurrency, has experienced significant price appreciation since its inception. Its price reached an all-time high of over $60,000 in April 2021, compared to less than $1 in its early days.
- According to a survey conducted by the Cambridge Centre for Alternative Finance, the number of cryptocurrency users worldwide reached 101 million in 2020, representing a significant increase from the 35 million users reported in 2018.
- The global remittance market, which involves the transfer of money across borders, is estimated to be worth over $700 billion. Cryptocurrencies have the potential to disrupt this market by offering faster and cheaper cross-border transactions.

The increasing popularity of cryptocurrencies and their potential impact on the global financial system are highlighted by these statistics and data points.

The rapid growth and adoption of cryptocurrencies in recent years have sparked a wide range of discussions and debates regarding their benefits and risks. The benefits and risks of crypto investing will be outlined in depth here, with case studies to back up the analysis through concrete examples and relevant statistics.

1.1.2 Benefits of Crypto Investing

a. Potential for High Returns: Cryptocurrencies have gained a reputation for their potential to deliver significant returns on investment. Bitcoin's price has appreciated significantly since its creation, enabling investors to earn substantial profits. Altcoins, which are other digital currencies, have also been shown to possess the potential for significant price appreciation.

b. Diversification: Cryptocurrencies offer investors the opportunity to diversify their investment portfolio. Traditional investments such as stocks and bonds can be affected by factors specific to the traditional financial system. Unlike traditional market risks, cryptocurrencies can offer exposure to a different asset class.

c. Technological innovation: Cryptocurrencies are based on blockchain technology, which has the potential to revolutionize various industries. People can benefit from investing in cryptocurrencies to support the development and utilization of new technologies such as Decentralized Finance (DeFi), NFT, and Blockchain-based Applications.

d. Accessibility and Inclusivity: Unlike traditional financial markets, cryptocurrency markets are open 24/7, allowing individuals from all over the world to participate at any time. Furthermore, cryptocurrencies have the potential to offer financial services to underprivileged and unbanked individuals through secure and efficient financial transactions.

1.1.2.1 Case Study: The Rise of Ethereum

Ethereum, the second-largest cryptocurrency by market capitalization, has gained significant attention for its smart contract functionality and its role in enabling decentralized applications (dApps). The growth of Ether (ETH), the native cryptocurrency for Ethereum, has been substantial and has yielded significant gains for early investors. Ethereum's emergence has led to the creation of a dynamic ecosystem of decentralized exchanges and finance platforms. This case study highlights the potential of investing in cryptocurrencies that enable innovative technologies and applications.

1.1.3 Risks of Crypto Investing

a. Volatility: Cryptocurrencies are known for their high volatility, with prices often experiencing significant fluctuations within short periods. This level of volatility can yield substantial profits, but also exposes investors to the possibility of significant losses. It is important for investors to carefully assess their risk tolerance and consider the potential impact of price volatility on their investment portfolios.

b. Regulatory Uncertainty: The regulatory landscape surrounding cryptocurrencies is still evolving in many jurisdictions. Changes in regulations or the introduction of new regulations can have a significant impact on the value and viability of cryptocurrencies. Investors should be cognizant of the uncertainty that comes with regulatory decisions and keep themselves informed about any changes in their timeline.

c. Security Risks: While cryptocurrencies utilize advanced cryptographic techniques to secure transactions, the overall security of the cryptocurrency ecosystem is not immune to risks.

Large sums of crypto have vanished due to hacking incidents, phishing attacks, and vulnerabilities in smart contracts. It is crucial for investors to adopt best practices in securing their cryptocurrency holdings, such as using hardware wallets and following proper security protocols.

d. Market Manipulation: Cryptocurrency markets are relatively young and less regulated compared to traditional financial markets. This lack of regulation can make cryptocurrency markets susceptible to manipulation, including pump-and-dump schemes, insider trading, and market manipulation through social media. Investors should be cautious and conduct thorough research before investing.

1.1.3.1 Case Study: The Mt. Gox Hack

The Mt. Gox exchange, once the largest Bitcoin exchange in the world, suffered a significant security breach in 2014, resulting in the loss of approximately 850,000 bitcoins. It also highlighted the security risks of cryptocurrencies, including potential massive losses from hacking and cyber-attacks.

Ultimately, there are several advantages to investing in crypto, such as high returns, diversification, involvement in technological advancements, and increased accessibility. It also has risks such as price instability, regulatory uncertainty and security risks, and market manipulation. It is important for investors to carefully consider these factors and conduct thorough research before engaging in crypto investing.

1.2 Why Invest in Cryptocurrencies?

This section aims to provide readers with a comprehensive

understanding of the reasons why investing in cryptocurrencies can be a lucrative opportunity.

One of the primary reasons to invest in cryptocurrencies is the potential for high returns on investment. Over the past decade, cryptocurrencies like Bitcoin and Ethereum have experienced significant price appreciation, creating wealth for early investors. This has attracted the attention of both individual investors and institutional players, contributing to the growth of the cryptocurrency market.

Also, the use of cryptocurrencies can facilitate the expansion of investment portfolios. Traditional asset classes, such as stocks and bonds, are often affected by similar economic factors. On the other hand, cryptocurrencies have relatively low correlations with traditional assets, making them an attractive option for diversifying an investment portfolio.

The growing adoption of cryptocurrency in various industries is another reason to invest. Major companies like Microsoft, PayPal and Tesla have started accepting cryptocurrencies as payment. This acceptance shows the perception of cryptocurrencies as a legal and fundamental asset class.

In addition, cryptocurrencies play a crucial role in the digital economy. The use of cryptocurrencies is driving online transactions and the rise of electronic commerce, making them a secure and efficient way to conduct digital transactions. As the digital economy continues to grow, it is expected that the demand for cryptocurrencies will increase, and their value will increase. In addition, investing in cryptocurrencies allows individuals to participate in technological innovations. Cryptocurrencies are based on blockchain technology, which has the potential to revolutionize various industries. For example, decentralized finance (DeFi) platforms use blockchain technology to provide financial services without the need for an intermediary. This innovation has the potential to revolutionize traditional financial systems and create new opportunities for investors. In addition, cryptocurrencies offer accessibility and coverage. Unlike traditional financial markets that operate within specific hours, cryptocurrency markets are open 24/7, allowing individuals from all over the world to participate at any time. This accessibility enables investors to take advantage of market opportunities and make informed investment decisions.

To illustrate the potential of investing in cryptocurrencies, let's explore a case study: the rise of Ethereum. Ethereum is the second-largest cryptocurrency by market capitalization and is known for its smart contract functionality. The inclusion of decentralized applications (dApps) has enabled Ethereum to produce a d ynamic ecosystem of innovative projects.

Investing in Ethereum early on has provided significant returns for investors. For instance, in 2015, the price of Ethereum was around $0.50 per Ether (ETH). As of [insert date], the price has increased to [insert current price], representing a remarkable appreciation in value. Investments in cryptocurrencies can yield substantial returns, as evidenced by this case study of pioneering technologies and applications.

There are many good reasons to invest in cryptocurrencies, but the risks can be significant. One of the primary risks is the high volatility of cryptocurrency prices. Cryptocurrencies are known for their price fluctuations, which can be substantial within short periods. For instance, Bitcoin (the most valuable cryptocurrency) has undergone several price fluctuations, reached all-time highs and undergone significant correction.

This volatility can lead to substantial gains, but it also exposes investors to the risk of significant losses. It is important for investors to carefully assess their risk tolerance and consider the potential impact of price volatility on their investment portfolios. Diversifying the portfolio with other asset classes can help mitigate this risk.

Regulatory uncertainty in the cryptocurrency space is another potential risk. What are the implications? Regulation in many jurisdictions remains fluid and changes, or the introduction of new regulations can have a significant impact on the value and viability of cryptocurrencies. For example, regulatory actions by governments can affect the acceptance and usage of cryptocurrencies, potentially impacting their value. Investors should stay informed about regulatory developments and consider the potential risks associated with regulatory uncertainty.

The security risks associated with cryptocurrencies are significant, but the cryptocurrency ecosystem poses significant threats to its overall operations. Hacking incidents, phishing attacks, and vulnerabilities in smart contracts have resulted in the loss of significant amounts of cryptocurrency. For example, the Mt. Gox exchange hack in 2014 resulted in the loss of approximately 850,000 bitcoins, highlighting the security risks associated with cryptocurrencies.

To mitigate security risks, investors should adopt best practices in securing their cryptocurrency holdings. This includes using hardware wallets, which provide an extra layer of security by storing private keys offline and following proper security protocols such as enabling two-factor authentication and regularly updating software.

Market manipulation is a potential drawback of

cryptocurrency markets due to their lack of regulation. Cryptocurrency markets are relatively young and less regulated compared to traditional financial markets. This lack of regulation can make cryptocurrency markets vulnerable to manipulation, including pump-and-dump schemes, insider trading, and market manipulation through social media. Investors should exercise caution and conduct thorough research before making investment decisions. Many people have embraced cryptocurrencies as an investment opportunity because of the potential for high returns and diversification, along with their technological advancements, ease in access, and inclusivity. However, it is essential to consider the risks involved, such as price volatility, regulatory uncertainty, security risks, and market manipulation.

Cryptocurrencies offer the potential for high returns on investment, as exemplified by the case study of Ethereum. Early investments in Ethereum have resulted in a significant increase in value, indicating that investing in these cryptocurrencies can yield substantial profits.

On the other hand, the high volatility of cryptocurrency prices is a significant risk to consider. Cryptocurrencies are known for their price fluctuations, which can be substantial within short periods. While volatility can lead to gains, it also exposes investors to the risk of significant losses. Investors should carefully assess their risk tolerance and consider diversifying their portfolios with other asset classes to mitigate this risk.

Regulatory uncertainty is another risk that investors should be aware of. Regulatory changes are still ongoing, and the value of or support of cryptocurrencies can be significantly affected by such changes. Investors should stay informed about regulatory developments and consider the potential risks associated with regulatory uncertainty.

Despite the use of advanced cryptographic techniques in cryptocurrency transactions, there are still significant security risks associated with these digital currencies. Hacking incidents, phishing attacks, and vulnerabilities in smart contracts have resulted in the loss of significant amounts of cryptocurrency. The use of hardware wallets, two-factor authentication, and software updates are all recommended practices for investors to ensure their investments are secure.

In addition, cryptocurrency markets are not subject to any type of market manipulation due to their lack of regulation. Due to their youthfulness and lack of regulation, cryptocurrency markets are susceptible to manipulation, including pump-and-dump schemes, insider trading, and social media manipulation. Investors should exercise caution, conduct thorough research, and rely on reputable sources of information before making investment decisions.

Investing in cryptocurrencies can be advantageous due to their potential for high returns, diversification, technological advancement, accessibility,
and inclusion in the market. However, it is crucial to consider the risks involved, including price volatility, regulatory uncertainty, security risks, and market manipulation. By understanding and mitigating these risks, investors can make informed investment decisions in the cryptocurrency market. In addition to the potential benefits and risks of investing in cryptocurrencies, it is important to approach cryptocurrency investments with a long-term perspective. Cryptocurrency markets can be highly volatile in the short term, but over time, they have shown potential for growth and technological advancement.

In order to make informed decisions about investing in cryptocurrencies, it is essential that we conduct thorough research and consult with financial experts to understand the market's current state. Diversification is also key, as it helps to spread the risk across different assets and reduces the impact of volatility.

It is crucial to establish a distinct investment plan and remain committed to it, rather than being affected by immediate market fluctuations. This includes setting realistic goals, determining an appropriate risk tolerance, and regularly reviewing and adjusting the investment portfolio as needed.

To sum up, it is crucial to keep abreast of market trends and regulatory updates in the cryptocurrency industry. By staying updated, investors can make informed decisions and adapt their strategies accordingly.

Investing in cryptocurrencies can be a rewarding venture, but it comes with risks. By being aware of these risks and taking steps to minimize their impact, investors can potentially take advantage of the potential opportunities presented by cryptocurrencies.

1.3 Benefits and Risks of Crypto Investing

Investing in cryptocurrencies comes with its own set of advantages and risks.

One of the key benefits of crypto investing is the ability to bypass intermediaries. The presence of various intermediaries, such as banks and payment processors, in conventional financial systems can lead to delays and increased costs. Cryptocurrencies enable direct peer-to-peer transactions, eliminating the need for intermediaries and reducing transaction costs.

Moreover, cryptocurrencies could be an asset to facilitate financial inclusion. In many parts of the world, traditional banking services are inaccessible to a significant portion of the population. The availability of cryptocurrencies allows anyone with internet access to participate in the global financial system, creating more chances for those who are not bankrupt or struggling.

The transparency of transactions is another advantage of crypto investing. Transparency and traceability are guaranteed in transactions made on the blockchain, making them available to anyone. This transparency helps to prevent fraud and corruption, as the transaction history is publicly available for scrutiny.

Investing in the digital currency also grants worldwide availability. Unlike traditional financial systems that are limited by borders and regulations, cryptocurrencies can be accessed and traded by anyone with an internet connection. Investment opportunities are available to individuals in less developed countries due to the availability of global accessibility and level playing fields.

It is crucial to be aware of the potential hazards involved in investing in cryptocurrencies. One of the main risks is the high volatility of cryptocurrency prices. Cryptocurrencies are known for their price fluctuations, which can be significant and sudden. This volatility can lead to substantial gains, but it can also result in substantial losses if not managed properly.

Another risk is the regulatory uncertainty surrounding cryptocurrencies. The fact that cryptocurrencies operate in a space beyond the traditional financial system means they are frequently subject to government and regulatory scrutiny. Changes in regulations and policies can have a significant impact on the value and usability of cryptocurrencies, making it important for investors to stay informed and adapt accordingly.

Security is also a concern in the crypto space. While blockchain technology provides inherent security features, such as encryption and decentralization, the risk of hacks and cyber-attacks is still present. Investors need to take precautions to protect their digital assets, such as using secure wallets and following best practices for secure transactions.

Also, the absence of well-established valuation models for cryptocurrencies can make it difficult to determine their intrinsic value. Unlike traditional assets that can be valued based on earnings or cash flows, cryptocurrencies often rely on market sentiment and speculation for their value. This can lead to market inefficiencies and increased price volatility.

Ultimately, there are several advantages to investing in cryptocurrencies, such as the potential for high returns, wider diversification, greater financial freedom, and increased transparency. However, it is crucial to be aware of the risks involved, including price volatility, regulatory uncertainties, security concerns, and the lack of established valuation models. Understanding these risks and making informed investment choices can help individuals navigate the world of cryptocurrency investing more effectively and potentially benefit from its opportunities. Investing in cryptocurrencies has gained significant popularity in recent years due to its potential benefits. The subsequent part will provide a detailed overview of the advantages and disadvantages of investing in crypto, along with supplementary information.

One of the key benefits of crypto investing is the ability to bypass intermediaries. Traditional financial systems often involve multiple intermediaries, such as banks and payment processors, which can result in delays and additional costs. Cryptocurrencies enable direct peer-to-peer transactions, eliminating the need for intermediaries and reducing transaction costs. According to a study conducted by Deloitte, blockchain technology has the potential to reduce global financial services infrastructure costs by up to $20 billion per year by 2022.

Furthermore, cryptocurrencies have the potential to enhance financial sustainability. Traditional banking services are not accessible to many people in various parts of the globe. With cryptocurrencies, anyone with internet access can participate in the global financial system, opening opportunities for individuals who are unbanked or underbanked. According to the World Bank, there are approximately 1.7 billion adults worldwide who are unbanked, and cryptocurrencies can provide them with access to financial services.

The transparency of transactions is another advantage of crypto investing. Blockchain technology allows for transparent and traceable transactions, as every transaction is recorded on the blockchain and can be accessed by anyone. This transparency helps to prevent fraud and corruption, as the transaction history is publicly available for scrutiny. According to a report by PwC, blockchain technology has the potential to add $1.76 trillion to the global economy by 2030 through various applications, including transparent supply chains and efficient government services.

Additionally, investing in cryptocurrencies provides the

opportunity for global accessibility. Unlike traditional financial systems that are limited by borders and regulations, cryptocurrencies can be accessed and traded by anyone with an internet connection. This global accessibility opens investment opportunities to individuals in countries with limited financial infrastructure and provides a level playing field for investors worldwide. According to a report by Cambridge Centre for Alternative Finance, the number of verified cryptocurrency users has grown from 35 million in 2018 to 101 million in 2020.

However, it is important to recognize and understand the risks associated with crypto investing. One of the main risks is the high volatility of cryptocurrency prices. Cryptocurrencies are known for their price fluctuations, which can be significant and sudden. This volatility can lead to substantial gains, but it can also result in substantial losses if not managed properly. According to Coinmarketcap, the total market capitalization of cryptocurrencies reached its peak at $2.5 trillion in May 2021, but it also experienced significant market corrections and fluctuations throughout its history.

Another risk is the regulatory uncertainty surrounding cryptocurrencies. As cryptocurrencies operate outside the traditional financial system, they often face regulatory challenges and scrutiny from governments and regulatory bodies. Changes in regulations and policies can have a significant impact on the value and usability of cryptocurrencies, making it important for investors to stay informed and adapt accordingly. According to a report by the International Monetary Fund (IMF), as of 2020, only about 25% of countries have comprehensive regulations in place for cryptocurrencies.

Security is also a concern in the crypto space. While blockchain technology provides inherent security features, such as encryption and decentralization, the risk of hacks and cyber-attacks is still present. Investors need to take precautions to protect their digital assets, such as using secure wallets and following best practices for secure transactions. According to a report by CipherTrace, losses from cryptocurrency hacks, scams, and frauds amounted to $1.9 billion in 2020.

Also, the absence of well-established valuation models for cryptocurrencies can make it difficult to determine their intrinsic value. Unlike traditional assets that can be valued based on earnings or cash flows, cryptocurrencies often rely on market sentiment and speculation for their value. This can lead to market inefficiencies and increased price volatility. According to a study conducted by the National Bureau of Economic Research, factors such as investor sentiments, market liquidity, and regulatory news can lead to significant fluctuations in cryptocurrencies.

Despite these risks, cryptocurrencies have shown the potential for high returns. Bitcoin, the first and most popular cryptocurrency, has seen a significant increase in price since its launch. According to CoinMarketCap, the price of Bitcoin has increased from less than $0.01 in 2010 to more than $60,000 in 2021. Other cryptocurrencies such as Ethereum and Ripple have also seen significant price growth over the years.

Crypto investments also provide diversification. Opportunities for investors. A traditional investment portfolio usually consists of stocks, bonds, and other traditional assets. Adding cryptocurrencies to a portfolio can help spread risk and potentially increase returns. According to a study by Yale University, including cryptocurrencies in a traditional portfolio can improve risk-adjusted returns due to their low correlation with traditional assets.

In addition, crypto investing also allows for early investment. Fintech, supply chain management, and healthcare are among the industries that can be affected by cryptocurrencies and their underlying technologies like blockchain. Investing in promising blockchain projects or innovative cryptocurrencies at an early stage can provide significant returns if the projects succeed. For example, early investors in Ethereum, which introduced smart contracts to the blockchain, saw substantial returns as the platform gained popularity.

In terms of statistics, the total market capitalization of cryptocurrencies has grown significantly over the years. According to CoinMarketCap, the total market capitalization of cryptocurrencies exceeded $2.5 trillion in May 2021, compared to just $17 billion in 2017. This growth demonstrates the increasing interest and adoption of cryptocurrencies as an investment asset class.

It is crucial to exercise extreme caution when investing in crypto and conduct thorough research. Due to the nascent nature of the crypto market, there are also numerous risks and challenges to consider. It is crucial to be aware of potential scams, fraudulent projects, and market manipulation. Investors should also be mindful of their risk tolerance and invest only what they can afford to lose.

In summary, the many benefits of investing in cryptocurrencies include high
returns, diversification and other opportunities for investment across multiple platforms with significant potential for growth through adoption of digital currency. However, it is crucial to be aware of the risks involved, including price volatility, regulatory uncertainties, security concerns,

and the lack of established valuation models. Understanding these risks and making informed investment choices can help individuals navigate the world of cryptocurrency investing more effectively and potentially benefit from its opportunities.

The possibility of cryptocurrencies offering high returns, diversification, and financial inclusion makes investing in them an exciting prospect. However, it is important to approach it with caution and be aware of the risks involved.

The absence of earnings or cash flows as the basis for valuation distinguishes cryptocurrencies from traditional assets. Instead, their value is often driven by market sentiment and speculation. Insufficient market management can lead to significant gains and substantial losses due in part to market inefficiencies and fluctuating prices.

Despite the risks, cryptocurrencies have demonstrated the potential for high returns. Bitcoin, the first and most well-known cryptocurrency, has experienced significant price appreciation over the years. Other cryptocurrencies, such as Ethereum and Ripple, have also seen substantial growth. However, it is important to note that past performance is not indicative of future results, and the cryptocurrency market can be unpredictable.

One of the advantages of crypto investing is the diversification it offers. By adding cryptocurrencies to a traditional investment portfolio, investors can potentially reduce risk and enhance returns. Cryptocurrencies have a low correlation with traditional assets, which means their price movements are often independent of each other. This can help offset losses in traditional investments during market downturns.

Another advantage of crypto investing is the potential for early-stage investment opportunities. Blockchain technology, which underlies cryptocurrencies, has the potential to disrupt various industries. Investing in promising blockchain projects or innovative cryptocurrencies at an early stage can result in significant returns if those projects succeed. For example, early investors in Ethereum, which introduced smart contracts to the blockchain, saw substantial profits as the platform gained popularity.

The market capitalization of cryptocurrencies has undergone a significant surge over
the years, according to market statistics. This indicates a growing interest and adoption of cryptocurrencies as an investment asset class.
It should be noted, however, that this is a relatively new and evolving market with risks and challenges.

When investing in cryptocurrencies, it is important to

conduct thorough research and remain knowledgeable about the market.

The crypto space is prone to scams, fraudulent projects, and market manipulation. It is important to be cautious and only invest what you can afford to lose. Other factors to consider are regulatory uncertainty and security concerns. Staying updated on regulations and implementing security measures, such as using secure wallets and following best practices, can help protect your investments.

Ultimately, however, there are benefits to investing in cryptocurrencies (high returns, wider diversification, greater financial freedom, etc.).But it is also important to be aware of the risks involved, including price instability, regulatory uncertainty, security issues, and the lack of well-established valuation models. The comprehension of these risks and making informed investment choices can assist individuals in navigating the cryptocurrency investing landscape and potentially reap its benefits.

Chapter 2: Getting Started with Cryptocurrency Investments

2.0 Introduction

Investing in cryptocurrencies can be a lucrative opportunity for individuals looking to diversify their investment portfolio. Nonetheless, it is crucial to grasp the fundamentals and implement a systematic strategy to maximize potential benefits and minimize potential risks. In this chapter, we will delve into the key steps involved in getting started with cryptocurrency investments, including setting up a digital wallet, choosing the right cryptocurrencies to invest in, and understanding market trends and analysis.

A software application that facilitates the safe storage, transmission, and reception of cryptocurrencies is known as a digital wallet. Setting up a digital wallet is the first step towards participating in the cryptocurrency market. In this section, we will provide a comprehensive guide on how to set up a digital wallet, covering the following aspects:

I. Hardware Wallets: These physical devices offer enhanced security by keeping the private keys offline. Examples include Ledger Nano S and Trezor.
II. Software Wallets: These wallets run on desktop or mobile devices and can be further categorized into hot wallets (connected to the internet) and cold wallets (offline storage).
III. Online Wallets: These wallets are web-based and allow easy access from any device with an internet connection. Examples include Coinbase and Binance.
IV. Research and choose a suitable wallet based on security, convenience, and supported cryptocurrencies.
V. Download and install the wallet application or create an online wallet account.
VI. Generate a new wallet address and securely store the private key or seed phrase.
VII. Enable two-factor authentication for added security.
VIII. Test the wallet by sending and receiving a small amount of cryptocurrency.

The abundance of cryptocurrencies available in the market necessitates extensive research and thorough analysis before investing. Cryptocurrencies have gained

significant popularity in recent years, attracting attention from both individual investors and institutional players. Due to the
high returns associated with their decentralized status, cryptocurrencies have become increasingly attractive as an investment vehicle. However, the volatile nature of the cryptocurrency market and the complex underlying technology can make it daunting for beginners to get started.

A digital wallet is a software application that allows individuals to securely store, send, and receive cryptocurrencies. Setting up a digital wallet is the first step towards participating in the cryptocurrency market.

This section will detail the steps involved in creating a digital wallet, along with the various types of digital currencies that can be used. Each type has its own advantages and security measures. Hardware wallets, such as Ledger Nano S and Trezor, offer enhanced security by keeping the private keys offline. Software wallets, on the other hand, run on desktop or mobile devices and can be further categorized into hot wallets (connected to the internet) and cold wallets (offline storage). Online wallets, such as Coinbase and Binance, are web-based and allow easy access from any device with an internet connection.

To set up a digital wallet, it is essential to research and choose a suitable wallet based on security, convenience, and supported cryptocurrencies. Once chosen, the next steps include downloading and installing the wallet application or creating an online wallet account. Creating a new wallet address and securely saving the private key or seed phrase is also important. Additionally, enabling two-factor authentication adds an extra layer of security. Finally, testing the wallet by sending and receiving a small amount of cryptocurrency ensures that the wallet is functioning correctly.

Before investing in one or more of these thousands of cryptocurrencies, you really need to research and study thoroughly. This section will provide detailed insights on how to choose the right cryptocurrencies to invest in, considering the following factors:

To assess the potential for long-term success, it is essential to evaluate the underlying technology of a cryptocurrency, such as blockchain. Factors like scalability, security, and the consensus mechanism of the blockchain network play a crucial role in determining the viability of a cryptocurrency. Researching the development team and their track record is also crucial in ensuring that the project's roadmap is delivered.

The market capitalization of a cryptocurrency is indicative of its popularity and potential for further development. Higher liquidity allows for easier buying and selling, making it an important factor to consider when choosing cryptocurrencies to invest in.

The real-world use case and adoption potential of a cryptocurrency must be evaluated. Look for partnerships, collaborations, and integrations with established companies or industries. A cryptocurrency with a strong use case and widespread adoption is more likely to experience long-term growth.

It is essential to be knowledgeable about the regulations go verning digital currencies in various countries. Regulatory changes can have a significant impact on the potential growth and adoption of a cryptocurrency. The regulatory risks of a particular cryptocurrency should also be considered before investment.

Investing in cryptocurrencies comes with inherent risks. Evaluating the risks associated with a particular cryptocurrency, such as market volatility, technological vulnerabilities, and regulatory uncertainties, is essential. Diversifying one's cryptocurrency portfolio across different cryptocurrencies can help mitigate some of these risks.

To make informed investment decisions in the cryptocurrency market, it is crucial to understand market trends and conduct thorough analysis.

The main concepts and instruments for studying

cryptocurrency markets are discussed in this section, where technical analysis focuses on analyzing historical price and volume data to identify patterns. Charting tools and indicators, such as moving averages, RSI, and MACD, are commonly used to analyse price movements and make predictions about future price movements. Understanding technical analysis can help investors identify entry and exit points for their trades.

Fundamental analysis is the process of determining the intrinsic value of cryptocurrency, considering factors such as the team, technology, partnerships, and market demand. This analysis helps investors assess whether a cryptocurrency is undervalued or overvalued and make investment decisions based on its potential for long-term growth.

Sentiment analysis is based on the use of social media, news stories, and other sources to gauge the general sentiment towards a specific cryptocurrency. Positive sentiment can indicate potential upward price movements, while negative sentiment may suggest a bearish market sentiment. Sentiment analysis can help investors understand market psychology and make informed decisions.

The cryptocurrency market demands regular updates from investors to stay abr east of developments. News about regulatory changes, technological advancements, partnerships, and market trends can have a significant impact on cryptocurrency prices.

Keeping up with industry experts and contributing to investment news can be advantageous for investors.

A well-planned risk management strategy is necessary when investing in the crypto space due to inherent risks. This section will cover key principles of risk management and security measures that investors should consider, including:

Diversifying one's cryptocurrency portfolio across different cryptocurrencies and asset classes can help spread the investment risk. Investing in a variety of cryptocurrencies with different use cases and market capitalizations can help mitigate the impact of price volatility on the overall portfolio.

Setting realistic investment goals and understanding one's risk appetite is crucial. Cryptocurrency investments can be highly volatile, and investors should be prepared for potential price fluctuations. Understanding one's risk tolerance and investing only what one can afford to lose can help manage emotional stress during market downturns.

Ensuring the security of one's digital assets is of utmost

importance. Implementing secure storage solutions, such as hardware wallets or cold storage, can protect cryptocurrencies from online threats and hacking attempts. Using strong and unique passwords, enabling two-factor authentication, and regularly updating software and firmware are essential security practices.

Monitoring the performance of one's cryptocurrency investments and regularly reviewing the portfolio is important. Keeping track of market trends, news, and any changes in the cryptocurrency ecosystem can help investors make informed decisions and take appropriate actions to maximize returns and minimize risks.

Getting started with cryptocurrency investments requires careful planning, research, and understanding of the market dynamics. This chapter has provided a comprehensive guide, covering the essential steps involved in setting up a digital wallet, choosing the right cryptocurrencies to invest in, understanding market trends and analysis, and implementing risk management and security measures. By following these guidelines and staying informed, individuals can navigate the cryptocurrency market with confidence and increase their chances of success.

2.1 Understanding the Technology

Cryptocurrencies have gained significant attention due to their underlying technology, blockchain. Evaluating the technology is crucial to assess the potential for long-term success of a cryptocurrency. Let's begin with a comprehensive explanation of blockchain technology, including its flexibility, security, consensus-building capabilities, and the importance of conducting research on the development team.

2.1.1 Evaluating the Underlying Technology

Blockchain is a decentralized digital ledger that records transactions across multiple computers. Its transparency and immutability make it an attractive technology for various use cases. For example, Ethereum, a popular blockchain platform, enables the execution of smart contracts, which have revolutionized decentralized applications (DApps).

To assess the potential of a cryptocurrency, we must evaluate the blockchain technology it is built upon. Consider Bitcoin, the first and most popular cryptocurrency. The Bitcoin blockchain has demonstrated remarkable stability and security since its inception in 2009. Its decentralized nature and robust consensus mechanism, Proof-of-Work (PoW), has enabled

Bitcoin to become a trusted and censorship-resistant digital currency. Another interesting point is this. Ripple uses a different consensus mechanism called the Ripple Protocol Consensus Algorithm (RPCA). This mechanism allows for faster transaction verification and scalability making it suitable for cross-border payments. By studying the underlying technology of cryptocurrency, we can determine its potential for long-term success.

2.1.2 Scalability, Security and Consensus Mechanisms

Scalability is an important issue for blockchain networks. As the number of transactions increases, the network must handle the load efficiently. For example, Bitcoin has faced scalability issues due to its limited block size. To solve this problem, solutions like the Lightning Network have been proposed, which allow faster off-chain transactions. On the other hand, Ethereum is actively working on Ethereum 2.0, which aims to improve scalability by implementing shading. Shading allows the network to process transactions in parallel, greatly increasing its capacity.

Security is critical in blockchain networks. The immutability of transactions and the decentralized nature of the blockchain make it immune to manipulation and fraud. However, vulnerabilities still exist. For example, in 2016, a vulnerability in Ethereum's smart contract code led to the infamous DAO hack, resulting in the theft of millions of dollars. This incident highlighted the importance of rigorous code review and security measures when building decentralized applications.

Consensus mechanisms determine how transactions are approved and added to the blockchain. In addition to PoW and RPCA, other mechanisms such as Proof-of-Stake (PoS) and Delegated Proof-of-Stake (DPoS) have also emerged. PoS allows network participants to stake their cryptocurrency holdings to validate transactions, while DPoS relies on selected delegates to confirm transactions.
The efficiency of these mechanisms is enhanced by their a bility to process transactions at higher speeds and consume less energy than PoW.

2.1. 3 Researching the Development Team

The development team behind a cryptocurrency project plays a crucial role in its success. Assessing their track record, expertise, and transparency is essential. For example, Cardano, a blockchain platform, is known for its scientific approach to development and its team's extensive research background. This has instilled confidence in Cardano's community.

On the other hand, the development team of Bitconnect, a now defunct cryptocurrency project, failed to deliver on its promises. The team was criticized for running a ponzi scheme, leading to significant financial losses for investors. Researching and evaluating the development team's credibility can help assess the project's potential for long-term success.

Ultimately, the technology behind a cryptocurrency is of great importance in determining its potential for long-term success. Evaluating the underlying blockchain technology, considering scalability, security, and consensus mechanisms, and researching the development team are essential steps in this process.

By examining the blockchain technology of a cryptocurrency, we can gain insights into its capabilities and limitations. For example, Bitcoin's blockchain has proven to be resilient and secure, while Ripple's blockchain offers faster transaction confirmations. Understanding these technologies allows us to assess their potential for widespread adoption and long-term success.

Scalability is a key consideration for blockchain networks, as they need to handle increasing transaction volumes efficiently. Bitcoin's limited block size has led to scalability issues, but solutions such as the Lightning Network have been proposed to address this issue. Ethereum's upcoming upgrade to Ethereum 2.0 aims to significantly improve scalability by implementing shading. Given the scalability potential of cryptocurrencies, this is critical to their use and adoption.

Security is critical in blockchain networks because they rely on decentralization and immutability to ensure trust. However, vulnerabilities can still exist, as seen in the DAO hack on Ethereum. To minimize these risks, careful code reviews and robust security measures are essential. Assessing a cryptocurrency's security measures provides insights into its resilience against potential threats.

Consensus mechanisms determine how transactions are validated and added to the blockchain. Understanding the consensus mechanism used by a cryptocurrency is crucial, as it impacts transaction speed, energy consumption, and decentralization. Proof-of-work, proof-of-stake, and delegated proof-of-stake are some of the commonly used mechanisms. Evaluating the consensus mechanism helps us assess a cryptocurrency's efficiency, sustainability, and governance structure.

Analysing the development team of a cryptocurrency project can help determine its credibility
and deliverables by conducting research on them. A team with a strong track record, expertise, and transparency inspires confidence in the project's potential for success. In contrast, Bitconnect projects, which have questi

onable development teams and deceitful practices, emphasize the importance of conducting due diligence on the team's credibility.

Briefly speaking, the understanding of cryptocurrency technology involves scrutinizing the underlying blockchain technology, considering its scalability, security, and consensus mechanisms in detail over time, as well information about the development team. These steps provide valuable insights into a cryptocurrency's potential for long-term success and adoption. By conducting thorough analysis and considering relevant examples and case studies, we can make informed decisions in the ever-evolving world of cryptocurrencies.

2.2 Market Capitalization and Liquidity

Here will be considering market capitalization, which reflects the total value of a cryptocurrency and can provide insights into its popularity and potential for growth, and the liquidity of a cryptocurrency, as higher liquidity allows for easier buying and selling.

2.2.1 Market Capitalization

Market capitalization is a measure of the total value of a cryptocurrency. It is calculated by multiplying the current price of a cryptocurrency by the total number of coins or tokens in circulation. The market capitalization of a cryptocurrency can provide insights into its popularity and potential for growth.

Example 1: Bitcoin (BTC) has a market capitalization of over $1 trillion, making it the largest cryptocurrency by market cap. This high market cap indicates Bitcoin's significant popularity and widespread adoption.

Example 2: Ethereum (ETH) has a market capitalization of over $300 billion. Although it is smaller than Bitcoin's market cap, it still represents a substantial value and highlights Ethereum's position as the second-largest cryptocurrency.

Example 3: Binance Coin (BNB) has experienced significant growth in market capitalization. In early 2021, its market cap surpassed $100 billion, making it one of the top cryptocurrencies. This growth can be attributed to the increasing popularity of the Binance exchange and the utility of BNB within the Binance ecosystem.

Example 4: Dogecoin (DOGE) gained attention in early 2021, primarily due to social media hype and endorsements from prominent individuals. While its market cap surged to billions of dollars, it is important to note that the market cap does not necessarily reflect the long-term value or stability of a cryptocurrency.

2.2.2 Liquidity

Liquidity refers to how easily a cryptocurrency can be bought or sold without significantly impacting its price. Higher liquidity is generally preferred as it allows for easier buying and selling, providing investors with more flexibility.

Example 1: Bitcoin (BTC) is known for its high liquidity. Due to its large market cap and widespread usage, there is a significant amount of buying and selling activity, making it easier to trade large volumes of Bitcoin without causing substantial price fluctuations.

Example 2: Tether (USDT) is a stable coin that is designed to maintain a value pegged to a fiat currency, such as the US dollar. It has high liquidity as it is widely used as a trading pair on many cryptocurrency exchanges, allowing users to quickly convert between cryptocurrencies and USDT.

Example 3: Ripple (XRP) is known for its high liquidity, with a substantial trading volume across various exchanges. This liquidity allows investors to easily buy and sell XRP without significant price impact. However, it is essential to consider regulatory factors and the ongoing legal proceedings surrounding Ripple.

Example 4: Uniswap (UNI) is a decentralized exchange built on the Ethereum blockchain. It has gained popularity for its liquidity pools, which enable users to provide liquidity and earn fees. The high liquidity of Uniswap allows for seamless swapping of tokens and contributes to its widespread usage.

These examples illustrate the importance of market capitalization and liquidity in cryptocurrency investing. Market cap can provide insights into a cryptocurrency's popularity and potential, while liquidity enables investors to easily buy or sell their assets.

In addition to market capitalization and liquidity, there are other important factors to consider when investing in cryptocurrencies. Let's explore some of these factors:

1. Technology and Innovation: Assess the underlying technology of a cryptocurrency and its potential for real-world applications. Look for projects that solve real problems or offer unique features that differentiate them from others in the market.

2. Development Team: Assess the expertise and experience of the development team behind the cryptocurrency. A strong team with a proven track record can inspire confidence in the long-term sustainability of the project.

3. Community and Adoption: Consider the size and engagement of the cryptocurrency community. A large and active community can contribute to the development and implementation of the project, providing valuable knowledge and support.

4. Regulatory Environment: Be aware of the regulatory landscape surrounding cryptocurrencies. Regulatory changes can have a significant impact on the value and legitimacy of certain cryptocurrency exchanges. Therefore, it is important to understand and comply with applicable laws.

5. Security: An assessment of the security measures implemented by the cryptocurrency project. Consider options such as efficient encryption, reliable storage facilities, and consistent security checks to minimize the risk of hacking or theft.

6. Partnerships and Integrations: Be aware of any strategic partnerships or integrations that cryptocurrency has established.
Establishing partnerships with reputable companies or platforms can enhance the credibility of the project and facilitate wider adoption.

7. Roadmap and Updates: View the project's roadmap and latest updates to understand its future and progress. By regularly reporting progress and completing milestones

, it shows that the team is committed to developing and growing the project.

8. Market Sentiment: Monitor general sentiment and trends in the cryptocurrency market. While the market's sentiment is subject to change, it can provide a glimpse into what people generally think and expect from cryptocurrencies.

It should be noted that investing in cryptocurrencies involves risks, such as the potential loss of capital. It's essential to diversify your portfolio, set realistic expectations, and only invest what you can afford to lose. Conduct thorough research, stay informed, and consult with financial professionals if needed. By considering these factors and taking a cautious and informed approach, you can navigate the cryptocurrency market more effectively.

Market capitalization and liquidity are crucial factors to consider when investing in cryptocurrencies. Let's explore more examples and case studies to further understand their significance:

These case studies demonstrate the practical applications of market capitalization and liquidity in cryptocurrency investing. However, it is important to conduct thorough research, consider other fundamental factors, and evaluate the overall market conditions before making investment decisions.

2.3 Use Case and Adoption

Cryptocurrency has revolutionized various industries by providing innovative use cases and adoption potential. Ethereum is an example of a decentralized platform that facilitates the development of smart contracts and distributed applications (DApps) With Ethereum, developers can build decentralized applications that eliminate the need for intermediaries and improve efficiency.

Another example is Ripple, a digital payment protocol designed for fast and low-cost cross-border transactions. Ripple's blockchain technology, coupled with its native cryptocurrency XRP, has gained significant adoption in the financial sector. Ripple's technology is being utilized by banks and remittance services worldwide to expedite and reduce international payments. This is advantageous.

Besides, other digital currencies such as Bitcoin have become popular as a means of holding value and avoiding inflation. Many investors view Bitcoin as digital gold due to its limited supply and decentralized nature. This use case has attracted institutional investors and individuals seeking to diversify their investment portfolios.

In terms of adoption, various industries have started integrating cryptocurrencies into their operations. For instance, the gaming industry has embraced cryptocurrencies as a means of in-game transactions and asset ownership. Games like Decentral and and Axie Infinity use non-fungible tokens (NFTs) to represent unique digital assets that can be bought, sold, and traded.

Additionally, the healthcare industry has shown interest in utilizing blockchain technology to securely store and share patient data. Companies like Medical chain is developing blockchain-based platforms that enable patients to have control over their medical records while ensuring privacy and security.

These examples highlight the diverse use cases and adoption potential of cryptocurrencies across different sectors. However, it's essential to consider the risks associated with crypto investing.

2.3.1 Analyse the real-world use case and adoption potential of a cryptocurrency

One cryptocurrency that exemplifies a real-world use case

and adoption potential is Chainlink (LINK). Chainlink aims to bridge the gap between blockchain technology and real-world data by providing secure and decentralized oracle services. Oracles are essential for smart contracts to interact with external data sources, making Chainlink a crucial component for the development of decentralized applications.

Chainlink has gained significant adoption in the decentralized finance (DeFi) space. DeFi platforms rely on accurate and reliable price data, and Chainlink's oracle network provides this crucial service. Decentralized lending, decentralized exchanges, and other DeFi applications can be built using Chainlink's secure integration of smart contracts with real-world data.

In addition, Chainlink's involvement with reputable companies and projects has increased its adoption rate. For example, Chainlink collaborated with Google Cloud to enable hybrid blockchain-cloud applications. This partnership allows developers to leverage Chainlink's oracle services on Google Cloud's infrastructure.

Chainlink has also integrated with prominent blockchain platforms like Ethereum and Polkadot, expanding its reach and adoption potential. These integrations enable developers on these platforms to access Chainlink's oracle network seamlessly.

2.3.2 Look for partnerships, collaborations, and integrations with established companies or industries

Cryptocurrencies that establish partnerships, collaborations, and integrations with established companies or industries often benefit from increased adoption and credibility.

One such example is VeChain (VET), a blockchain platform that focuses on supply chain management and product verification. VeChain has formed strategic partnerships with several leading companies, including PwC and DNV GL. Through these partnerships, VeChain can leverage the expertise and connections of these established companies, resulting in increased adoption within supply chain.

Another notable example is Binance Coin (BNB), the native cryptocurrency of the Binance exchange. Binance has integrated BNB into various aspects of its platform, creating a vibrant ecosystem around the token. BNB can be used to pay for trading fees on the Binance exchange, participate in token sales on the Binance Launchpad, and even book travel accommodations through Binance's partnership with Travala.

These examples demonstrate how partnerships, collaborations, and integrations with established companies or industries can contribute to the adoption and success of cryptocurrencies. The ability to network with existing networks and establish a strong foundation for users can be one of the ways in which cryptocurrencies can gain legitimacy.

However, it's important to note that investing in cryptocurrencies carries certain risks. The volatility of the crypto market is one significant risk factor. Prices of cryptocurrencies can experience significant fluctuations, leading to potential losses for investors.

Additionally, regulatory uncertainty is another risk to consider. Governments around the world are still developing regulations for cryptocurrencies, which can impact their adoption and legal status. Changes in regulations or government actions can have a substantial impact on the value and usability of cryptocurrencies.

Security is also a concern when investing in cryptocurrencies. While blockchain technology provides inherent security features, hackers and scammers are continuously looking for vulnerabilities and exploits. To ensure the protection of their digital assets, investors must utilize hardware wallets and follow best security practices.

In summary, there are numerous different ways in which cryptocurrencies can be employed and its adoption potential. From revolutionizing industries to forming partnerships with established companies, cryptocurrencies have the potential to reshape the way we transact and interact with digital assets.
To ensure your investment in cryptocurrencies, it's important to conduct thorough research and be aware of the potential risks.

2.4 Regulatory Environment

The regulatory landscape surrounding cryptocurrencies varies across jurisdictions.
Across different nations, digital currencies and blockchain technology have gained widespread acceptance while others have enforced strict regulations or even banned their utilization.

Example 1: United States
In the United States, cryptocurrencies are regulated by various agencies, such as the Securities and Exchange Commission (SEC) and the Commodity Futures Trading Commission (CFTC). The SEC regulates cryptocurrencies that are classified as securities, while the CFTC regulated cryptically traded commodities. Additiona

lly, individual states may have their own regulations and licensing requirements for cryptocurrency businesses.

Example 2: Japan
Japan has taken a more proactive approach to regulate cryptocurrencies. In 2017, the country recognized Bitcoin as a legal payment method and implemented a licensing framework for cryptocurrency exchanges. The Financial Services Agency (FSA) oversees the regulation of cryptocurrencies and has established guidelines for exchanges to ensure consumer protection and prevent money laundering.

Example 3: China
China has imposed strict regulations on cryptocurrencies. In 2017, the country banned Initial Coin Offerings (ICOs) and shut down domestic cryptocurrency exchanges. The government cited concerns about fraud, money laundering, and financial stability as reasons for the ban. The digital yuan, China's virtual currency, has been launched after exploring the potential of blockchain technology.

Now, let's delve into the impact of regulations on the potential growth and adoption of cryptocurrencies:

2.4.1 Impact of Regulations

Regulations play a significant role in shaping the growth and adoption of cryptocurrencies. Regulatory developments can either encourage innovation and investor confidence or hinder the growth of the crypto market.

Example 1: Positive Impact
Clear and well-defined regulations can provide a sense of security to investors and businesses operating in the crypto space. This can attract institutional investors who may have been hesitant due to regulatory uncertainty. In addition, regulations aimed at protecting consumers can boost trust and encourage the wider adoption of digital currencies.

Example 2: Negative Impact
Excessive regulations or bans can stifle innovation and drive cryptocurrency-related businesses to operate in jurisdictions with more favourable regulatory environments. Unclear or inconsistent regulations can create confusion and hinder the growth of the crypto market. Strict regulations may also limit the accessibility of cryptocurrencies to the public, inhibiting their adoption as a mainstream form of payment.

Understanding the regulatory landscape surrounding cryptocurrencies is crucial for investors and businesses in the crypto space. Regulations can have both positive and negative effects on the growth and adoption of cryptocurrencies. The presence of well-defined, transparent regulations can foster trust and lure institutional investors, whereas excessive regulations or bans can hinder the growth of the crypto market.

2.4.2 Assessing the Impact of Regulations on Growth and Adoption

When assessing the impact of regulations on the potential growth and adoption of a cryptocurrency, several factors come into play.

Example 1: Market Stability
Regulations that promote market stability can instil confidence in investors and encourage wider adoption of cryptocurrencies. Measures such as anti-money laundering (AML) and know-your-customer (KYC) requirements can help prevent illicit activities and protect investors.

Example 2: Innovation and Technology
Regulations that strike a balance between consumer protection and fostering innovation are crucial for the growth of the crypto market. Forward-thinking regulations that encourage the development of blockchain technology

and provide a supportive environment for start-ups can drive growth and adoption.

Example 3: Global Compatibility
The compatibility of regulations across jurisdictions is important for the global adoption of cryptocurrencies. Harmonization of regulations can facilitate cross-border transactions and encourage international collaboration in the crypto space.

Example 4: Investor Protection
Regulations that prioritize investor protection can enhance trust and confidence in cryptocurrencies. Measures such as requiring exchanges to implement robust security measures, ensuring transparency in token offerings, and establishing investor compensation schemes can mitigate risks and attract more investors.

Example 5: Regulatory Clarity
Clear and consistent regulations provide certainty for businesses and investors, enabling them to navigate the crypto market with confidence. Unclear or ambiguous regulations can create barriers and hinder the growth and adoption of cryptocurrencies.

Ultimately, the effects of regulations on the rise and adoption of cryptocurrencies are complex. Well-designed and balanced regulations can foster innovation, enhance investor protection, and promote wider adoption. However, excessive or inconsistent regulations can impede growth and drive businesses to more favourable regulatory environments. It is important for regulators to strike a balance between fostering innovation and protecting market participants to ensure the sustainable development of the crypto market.

2.5 Investment Risks

Investing in cryptocurrencies carries certain risks that investors should be aware of. These risks include market instability, technological weaknesses, and regulatory uncertainties. It is important to assess these risks and take appropriate measures to mitigate them.

2.5.1 Assessing the risks associated with a specific cryptocurrency

- Market analysis:
  One of the biggest risks associated with investing in cryptocurrency is market volatility. Cryptocurrencies are known for their price volatility, which is affected by various factors such as market sentiment, news and regulatory developments. Prices can experience significant price increases in a short period of time, making it a high-risk investment. For example, the

price of Bitcoin reached a record high of nearly $20,000 in 2017, only to drop to $3,000 in 2018. Investors should be prepared for such volatility and assess their risk tolerance before investing.

- Technological Vulnerabilities
Cryptocurrencies are built on blockchain technology, which is considered secure. Despite this, there are still opportunities for investments that can be compromised. For example, hackers can exploit weaknesses in the technology and steal funds from cryptocurrency wallets or exchanges. Additionally, software bugs or glitches can also lead to financial losses. It is important to choose reputable and secure platforms for trading and storing cryptocurrencies and to take necessary security precautions such as using strong passwords and enabling two-factor authentication.

- Regulatory Uncertainties
The regulatory landscape for cryptocurrencies is still evolving and can vary significantly from one jurisdiction to another. The value and acceptance of cryptocurrencies may be affected by uncertainty in terms of regulatory scrutiny. For example, governments may introduce new regulations that restrict or even ban certain cryptocurrencies, causing them to lose value. Investors should inform themselves about their eligibility criteria and

consider the potential impact on their investment.

Examples of risks:

1. Mt. Gox Hack: In 2014, Mt. Gox, one of the largest crypto exchanges at the time, suffered a major hack that resulted in the loss of approximately 850,000 bitcoins, worth more than $450 million at the time. This incident highlighted the vulnerability of centralized exchanges and the risks associated with the storage of funds on third-party platforms.

2. China's Cryptocurrency Ban: In 2017, China announced a ban on Initial Coin Offerings (ICOs) and cryptocurrency exchanges, causing a significant drop in prices of major cryptocurrencies. This regulatory action created uncertainty in the market and resulted in a decline in investor confidence.

2.5.2 Diversify investments across multiple cryptocurrencies to mitigate risk

Diversification is a widely recognized strategy in traditional investing, and it also applies to cryptocurrencies. By diversifying investments across multiple cryptocurrencies, investors can mitigate the risk associated with any cryptocurrency.

Cryptocurrencies can have different characteristics, market trends, and adoption rates. By investing in a diverse portfolio of cryptocurrencies, investors can potentially benefit from the growth of multiple projects while reducing the impact of any individual cryptocurrency's poor performance. This approach allows investors to spread their risk and increase the likelihood of generating positive returns.

For example, suppose an investor allocates their investment across Bitcoin, Ethereum, and Ripple. If the price of Bitcoin declines, but the prices of Ethereum and Ripple increase, the overall portfolio value may still grow. Diversification helps to balance out the volatility of individual cryptocurrencies and can provide a more stable investment strategy.

It is important to note that diversification does not eliminate all risks. The cryptocurrency market can still be subject to market-wide fluctuations and external factors that affect the entire industry. Investors should carefully research and evaluate the cryptocurrencies they wish to include in their portfolio, considering market
trends, technology choices, as well as team performance and community support.

Investing in cryptocurrencies can be a high-risk

venture due to factors such as market volatility, technological vulnerabilities, and regulatory uncertainties. Investors should carefully evaluate these risks and take appropriate measures to mitigate them.

The approach may involve dividing investments among various digital currencies to spread the risk and potentially profiting from
different project developments.

Market volatility is a significant risk in the cryptocurrency market. Prices can experience dramatic fluctuations within short periods of time, making it a challenging investment environment. For example, the price of Bitcoin reached nearly $20,000 in 2017 but dropped to around $3,000 in 2018. To ensure a risk-based investment, investors must be prepared for volatility.

Technological vulnerabilities also pose a risk to cryptocurrency investments. Hackers can exploit vulnerabilities in cryptocurrency wallets or exchanges that cause financial losses. In addition, software errors or malfunctions can
also cause damage to funds. It is important to choose reputable and secure platforms for trading and storing cryptocurrencies and
implement strict security measures such as two-

factor authentication.

Uncertainty of regulation increases the risk of investing in cryptocurrencies. The cryptocurrency regulatory landscape is still evolving and may vary from country to country. Governments may introduce new regulations that restrict or even ban certain cryptocurrencies, affecting their value and acceptance. Investors should stay informed about the regulations in their respective jurisdictions and consider the potential impact on their investments.

To mitigate risk, diversification is recommended. By investing in a diverse portfolio of cryptocurrencies, investors can reduce the impact of any individual cryptocurrency's poor performance. The various cryptocurrencies differ in their features, market dynamics, and usage patterns. For example, if the price of Bitcoin declines but the prices of Ethereum and Ripple increase, a diversified portfolio may still see overall growth. However, it is important to note that diversification does not eliminate all risks, as the cryptocurrency market can still be subject to market-wide fluctuations and external factors affecting the industry.

In summary, there are risks associated with putting your money into cryptocurrencies. Market volatility, technological vulnerability and regulatory uncertainty are important factors to consider. Diversifying investments across multiple cryptocurrencies can help minimize risk, but investors should do thorough research and consider various factors before making investment decisions.

Part 3: Understanding Market Trends and Analysis Make Informed Decisions Investing is important to understand and analyse market trends in the market. cryptocurrency industry. This section provides a detailed review of various market trends and analysis methods, including.

2.6 Technical Analysis

Technical analysis is a method used in investing and trading to evaluate and forecast future price movements based on historical price data, patterns, and indicators. The process entails scrutinizing price charts and employing investment tools and techniques to make informed investment choices. Technical analysis assumes that historical price patterns and trends can provide insights into future price movements.

2.6.1 Learn how to analyse price charts, patterns, and indicators to predict future price movements

Analysing price charts, patterns, and indicators is an essential aspect of technical analysis. By examining historical price data and identifying patterns and indicators, investors and traders can predict future price changes. Here are some key points to consider:

1. Price Chart Analysis: Price charts provide a visual representation of an asset's price movement over time. Different types of charts, such as candlesticks, charts, and bars, offer different levels of detail. These charts provide information on patterns, support and resistance levels, and important prices.

2. Trend Analysis: Trends are one of the basic concepts of technical analysis. They represent the general direction in which an asset's price is moving. Trends can be classified as uptrends (rising prices), downtrends (falling prices), or sideways trends (range-bound prices). Identifying the prevailing trend is crucial for making informed investment decisions.

3. Chart Patterns: Chart patterns are recurring formations in price charts that can indicate potential future price movements. Some common chart patterns include:

   I. Head and Shoulders: This pattern consists of a peak (head) with two smaller peaks (shoulders) on either side. It suggests a potential trend reversal from bullish to bearish.

II. Double Tops/Bottoms: A double top pattern occurs when an asset's price reaches a peak, retraces, and then reaches a similar peak again. This pattern indicates that the potential trend is changing from an uptrend to a downtrend. Conversely, a double bottom trend pattern indicates a potential trend reversal from bearish to bullish.

III. Triangles: Triangle patterns are formed by trend convergence and indicate a period of consolidation before a potential breakout. They can be symmetrical, ascending or descending depending on the slope of the trend lines.

4. Indicators: Technical indicators are mathematical calculations applied to price and volume data. They provide additional information about price movements and help traders confirm or confirm their analysis. Some commonly used indicators include:

- Moving Averages: Moving averages calculate the average price over a specific period. They smooth out price fluctuations and help identify the trend direction. Traders often use the crossover of different moving averages as a signal for potential buy or sell opportunities.

- Relative Strength Index (RSI): RSI measures the speed and change of price movements. It oscillates between 0 and 100 and indicates whether an asset is overbought or oversold. Traders can use RSI to identify potential trend reversals or divergence between price and momentum.
- Bollinger Bands: Bollinger Bands consist of a moving average with an upper and lower band that represents standard deviations from the average. They help identify periods of high or low volatility and potential price reversals.

By combining price chart analysis, pattern recognition, and the use of indicators, traders can develop a comprehensive technical analysis strategy to predict future price movements. It is important to note that technical analysis is not fool proof and should be used in conjunction with other forms of analysis and risk management techniques.

Remember, practice and experience are crucial in developing proficiency in technical analysis. Continuously studying price charts, observing patterns, and testing different indicators and strategies will enhance your skills and decision-making abilities in crypto investing.

2.6.2 Explore popular technical analysis tools and strategies, such as moving averages, RSI, and Fibonacci retracements

Price charts are graphical representations of historical price data over a specific period. They display the price movements of an asset over time, such as minutes, hours, days, weeks, or months. Candlestick charts, line charts, and bar charts are commonly used in technical analysis.

Technical analysis identifies recurring patterns in price charts that can indicate potential future price movements. Some common patterns include:

- Trend Patterns: Trend patterns show the direction of the market, whether it's in an uptrend (rising prices), downtrend (falling prices), or sideways trend (range-bound prices).

- Reversal Patterns: Reversal patterns indicate a potential change in the current trend. Examples include double tops/bottoms, head and shoulders, and bullish/bearish engulfing patterns.

- Continuation Patterns: Continuation patterns suggest that the existing trend is likely to continue after a brief consolidation. Examples include triangles, flags, and pennants.

3. Indicators: Technical analysis employs indicators to provide additional information about price movements and trends. These indicators are mathematical calculations applied to price and volume data. Some popular indicators include:

- Moving Averages: Moving averages smooth out price data over a specific period and help identify the trend direction. The most common types are simple moving averages (SMA) and exponential moving averages (EMA).

- Relative Strength Index (RSI): RSI measures the speed and change of price movements. It indicates whether an asset is overbought or oversold and can help identify potential trend reversals.

- Fibonacci Retracements: Fibonacci retracements use horizontal lines to indicate potential support and resistance levels based on the Fibonacci sequence. Traders use these levels to identify potential entry or exit points.

Examples:

1. Analysing Price Charts: Suppose you are analysing the price chart of a cryptocurrency and notice a clear uptrend with higher highs and higher lows. This indicates an uptrend, which means that the price may go higher soon. Based on this analysis, you can consider buying cryptocurrency.

2. Using moving averages: You watch the stock price consistently below its 50-day moving average, which indicates an uptrend. This can be a signal to enter a long position or hold an existing position.

3. Identifying Reversal Patterns: You will see a head and shoulder pattern forming on the price chart of the currency pair. This pattern suggests a potential trend reversal from an uptrend to a downtrend. Traders might consider selling or shorting the currency pair based on this pattern.

4. Applying Fibonacci Retracements: After a significant price increase, you use Fibonacci retracement levels to identify potential support levels where the price may bounce back. This can help determine optimal entry points for buying the asset.

The fundamental concept of technical analysis is to scrutinize price charts, identify patterns in them over time and use the indicators provided for future price fluctuations. By understanding these concepts and applying various tools and strategies, investors and traders can make more informed decisions in the crypto market.

2.6.3 Fundamental Analysis

Fundamental analysis is a key approach used in cryptocurrency investing to evaluate the intrinsic value of a digital asset. It involves analysing various factors that impact the value of cryptocurrencies, including the project's team, partnerships, adoption rate, and market demand. By understanding these fundamental factors, investors can make informed decisions about which cryptocurrencies to invest in.

2.6.4 Evaluating Fundamental Factors

To evaluate the fundamental factors that impact the value of cryptocurrencies, investors should consider the following:

1. Project's Team: The team behind a cryptocurrency

project plays a crucial role in its success. Investors should assess the team's experience, expertise, and track record. A strong team with a proven track record increases the likelihood of project success.

Example: When evaluating a cryptocurrency project, investors may consider the team's previous successful projects, their technical expertise, and their ability to execute the project's vision.

2. Partnerships: Partnerships can significantly influence the value of a cryptocurrency. Collaborations with established companies or organizations can enhance a project's credibility and increase its chances of widespread adoption.

Example: If a cryptocurrency project forms a partnership with a well-known technology company, it may indicate that the project has potential and could attract more investors.

3. Adoption Rate: The adoption rate refers to the rate at which a cryptocurrency is being used by individuals, businesses, or institutions. Higher adoption rates indicate a growing demand for the cryptocurrency, which can positively impact its value.

Example: If a cryptocurrency is being widely used for real-world transactions and has a large user base, it suggests that the project has gained significant traction and has the potential for future growth.

4. Market Demand: Understanding the market demand for a cryptocurrency is essential. Factors such as the utility of the cryptocurrency, its unique features, and its potential to solve real-world problems can drive demand and increase its value.

Example: A cryptocurrency that offers innovative solutions and addresses current market challenges may attract investors and experience increased demand.

2.6.5 Assessing the Whitepaper and Roadmap

To determine the viability of investing in the cryptocurrency project, it is necessary to evaluate its whitepaper and roadmap alongside fundamental factors.

1. Whitepaper: A cryptocurrency's whitepaper is a document that outlines the project's goals, technology, and implementation strategy. Investors should carefully read the whitepaper to understand what they want to achieve in terms of vision, technical details and potential issues.

Example: When assessing a cryptocurrency's whitepaper, investors may look for a clear problem statement, innovative solutions, and a well-defined roadmap for development.

2. Roadmap: A roadmap provides a timeline of the project's milestones and development phases. Investors should evaluate the feasibility of the roadmap and assess whether the project has a realistic plan for achieving its goals.

Example: If a cryptocurrency project has a detailed roadmap with achievable milestones and clear timelines, it suggests that the team has a well-thought-out plan for development.

2.7 Comparing with Similar Projects

To gain a better understanding of a cryptocurrency's potential, investors should consider the competitive landscape and compare the cryptocurrency with similar projects in the market.

1. Competitive Landscape: Analysing the competitive landscape helps investors identify the unique selling points and competitive advantages of a cryptocurrency project. This analysis can provide insights into how the project differentiates itself from its competitors.

Example: By analysing the competitive landscape, investors can identify whether a cryptocurrency project offers unique features or addresses a specific market niche that sets it apart from similar projects.

2. Comparative Analysis: Comparing a cryptocurrency project with similar projects can help investors assess its potential for success. Investors should consider factors such as market demand, team expertise, partnerships, and adoption rate when conducting a comparative analysis.

Example: If a cryptocurrency project has a comparative advantage over similar projects in terms of a strong team, strategic partnerships, and a high adoption rate, it may indicate a higher potential for success.

Case Study: Evaluating Fundamental Factors in Crypto Investing

Let's consider a case study to understand how fundamental analysis can be applied in cryptocurrency investing.

Case: XYZ Coin

XYZ Coin is a relatively new cryptocurrency project that aims to revolutionize the supply chain industry by using blockchain technology. As an investor, you are interested in evaluating the fundamental factors of XYZ Coin before making an investment decision.

1. Project Team: You research the team behind XYZ Coin and find that they have expertise in both blockchain

technology and the supply chain industry. Team members have previously worked on successful blockchain projects and have a deep understanding of the challenges facing the supply chain industry.

2. Partnerships: XYZ Coin has established strategic partnerships with major logistics companies and industry associations. These partnerships demonstrate that the project has gained recognition and support from key players in the supply chain industry.

3. Acceptance Fee: You will notice that XYZ Coin is already accepted by several major companies in the supply chain sector. These companies have started using XYZ Coin's blockchain platform to track and trace their products, leading to an increasing adoption rate.

4. Market Demand: The supply chain industry is facing challenges such as transparency issues and inefficient processes. XYZ Coin's solution addresses these challenges by providing a transparent and secure platform for supply chain management. This innovative solution has attracted attention and generated market demand for XYZ Coin.

Assessing the Whitepaper and Roadmap:

You carefully review XYZ Coin's whitepaper and find that it clearly outlines the project's goals, technology, and implementation strategy. The whitepaper demonstrates a deep understanding of the supply chain industry and presents a comprehensive roadmap for the development of XYZ Coin's blockchain platform.

Comparing with Similar Projects:

You compare XYZ Coin with other blockchain projects in the supply chain industry and find that XYZ Coin has unique features and a strong competitive advantage. While there are other projects addressing similar issues, XYZ Coin's strategic partnerships, growing adoption rate, and innovative solution set it apart from its competitors.

Based on your evaluation of the fundamental factors, you decide to invest in XYZ Coin. You believe that the project's strong team, strategic partnerships, growing adoption rate, and unique solution position it for long-term success in the supply chain industry.

Fundamental analysis is a vital component of investing in the cryptocurrency market. By evaluating factors such as the project's team, partnerships, adoption rate, market demand, whitepaper, roadmap, and competitive landscape, investors can make informed decisions and identify promising investment opportunities in the crypto market.

2.8 Sentiment Analysis

Sentiment analysis is a valuable tool for crypto investors as it allows them to gauge the overall market sentiment towards a particular cryptocurrency. Through social media, online forums, and newspaper articles alike, investors can gain insight into the attitudes of both parties involved in an investment decision-making process. This information can help investors make more informed decisions about their crypto investments.

Sentiment analysis techniques involve analysing the text to identify and quantify the emotions and opinions conveyed by the writer. Natural language processing (NLP) algorithms are commonly used in sentiment analysis to analyse text and determine sentiment. These algorithms can identify positive, negative, or neutral sentiments and can also detect specific emotions. Sentiment analysis plays a crucial role in crypto investing as it allows investors to gauge the overall market sentiment towards a particular cryptocurrency. By analysing social media platforms, online forums, and news articles, investors can gain insights into the sentiment of both investors and the public. In this section, we will explore sentiment analysis techniques and provide examples to illustrate their application in the context of crypto investing.

Sentiment analysis, also known as opinion mining, is a computational method used to determine the sentiment expressed in a piece of text. It involves analysing the text to identify and quantify the emotions and opinions conveyed by the writer. By understanding the sentiment behind the text, investors can make more informed decisions about their crypto investments.

One common technique used in sentiment analysis is the use of natural language processing (NLP) algorithms. These algorithms analyse the text to identify positive, negative, or neutral sentiments. They can also detect specific emotions such as excitement, fear, or optimism. NLP algorithms can be trained on large datasets of labelled text to improve their accuracy in identifying sentiment.

For example, let's say an investor is considering investing in Bitcoin. They can use sentiment analysis to gauge the overall sentiment towards Bitcoin by analysing social media posts, news articles, and online forums. By analysing the sentiment expressed in these sources, an investor can find out whether most people have a positive or negative opinion about Bitcoin. Here is an example to show how sentiment analysis is used in crypto investing:

Scenario: Investor A is considering investing in Ethereum. You want to understand the sentiment towards

Ethereum in the crypto community.

1. Social Media Analysis: Investor A uses sentiment analysis tools to analyse social media platforms like Twitter and Reddit. They collect a large sample of tweets and messages that mention Ethereum and analyse the sentiment expressed in these messages. A sentiment analysis tool classifies sentiment as positive, negative, or neutral. Based on the analysis, Investor A finds that most tweets and messages are positive, showing positive sentiment towards Ethereum in the crypto community.

2. Analysis of News Articles: Investor A also analyses Ethereum news articles using sentiment analysis techniques. They collect a sample of news articles from reputable sources and analyse the sentiment expressed in those articles. A sentiment analysis tool classifies sentiment as positive, negative, or neutral. Based on the analysis, Investor A finds that most news articles are positive, indicating a positive sentiment towards Ethereum in the media.

3. Online Forum Analysis: Lastly, Investor A analyses online forums dedicated to discussions about cryptocurrencies. They collect a sample of forum posts discussing Ethereum and analyse the sentiment expressed in these posts. The sentiment analysis tool categorizes the sentiment as positive, negative, or neutral. Based on the

analysis, Investor A finds that most forum posts are positive, indicating a positive sentiment towards Ethereum among crypto enthusiasts.

Based on the sentiment analysis results, Investor A concludes that there is a positive sentiment towards Ethereum in the crypto community. This information can help them make an informed decision about whether to invest in Ethereum.

In conclusion, sentiment analysis is a valuable tool in crypto investing as it allows investors to understand the sentiment of both investors and the public towards a particular cryptocurrency. By analysing social media platforms, online forums and news articles, investors can gain insights that can help them make their investment decisions. Sentiment analysis techniques, such as natural language processing algorithms, can help investors identify and categorize sentiment expressed in text, providing a valuable tool for crypto investors.

2.8.1 Learn sentiment analysis techniques to determine the overall market sentiment about a particular cryptocurrency

One method of sentiment analysis is the use of sentiment lexicons. Emotion dictionaries are databases that contain words and their values related to emotions. These values indicate the polarity of the words' emotions, whether positive or negative. The sentiment scores of the words in the text can be used by investors to determine the overall mood.

For example, let's say an investor wants to determine the sentiment towards a specific cryptocurrency like Ripple (XRP). Social media posts, news articles and online forums can be analysed using sentiment dictionaries. By calculating the sentiment scores of the words used to describe Ripple, the investor can determine whether the sentiment is positive, negative, or neutral.

Another sentiment analysis technique is the use of machine learning algorithms. These algorithms can be trained on labelled datasets to classify text into different sentiment categories. The algorithm is given texts that are already tagged with their sentiments during the training process. By learning patterns from labelled data, the algorithm can identify new texts and apply them to its own classification.

For instance, an investor may want to analyse social media posts about a specific cryptocurrency, such as Ethereum. They can use a machine learning algorithm to classify the sentiment of these posts. By training the algorithm on a dataset of labelled social media posts, where each post is labelled as positive, negative, or neutral, the algorithm can learn to classify new posts based on their sentiment.

2.8.2 Monitor social media platforms, online forums, and news articles to understand the sentiment of investors and the public

Social media platforms, online forums, and news articles are rich sources of information for understanding the sentiment of investors and the public towards cryptocurrencies. By monitoring these sources, investors can gain insights into the sentiment trends and make informed decisions about their investments.

For example, an investor may want to understand the sentiment towards a particular cryptocurrency, such as Bitcoin. They can monitor social media platforms like Twitter and Reddit, online forums dedicated to crypto discussions, and news articles related to Bitcoin. By analysing the sentiment expressed in the posts, comments, and articles, the investor can get a sense of whether the sentiment is positive, negative, or neutral.

Monitoring sentiment in real-time can also provide valuable insights. The use of sentiment analysis during significant events or announcements related to cryptocurrencies can assist investors in interpreting the market's immediate response. By analysing social media posts and news articles during these events, investors can identify any shifts in sentiment and adjust their investment strategies accordingly.

In the context of crypto investing, sentiment analysis is a powerful tool that can help investors understand their own feelings and those of others when it comes to what they're trading for. By exploring sentiment analysis techniques such as sentiment lexicons and machine learning algorithms, investors can gauge the overall market sentiment. Additionally, by monitoring social media platforms, online forums, and news articles, investors can gain real-time insights into sentiment trends and make more informed decisions about their crypto investments. Using sentiment analysis, investors can gain insight into market sentiment and identify patterns or trends that may impact their investment decisions.

To further illustrate the importance of sentiment analysis in crypto investing, let's consider a case study:

Case Study: Sentiment Analysis in Crypto Investing

Let's say an investor is considering investing in a relatively new cryptocurrency called XYZ Coin. Before deciding, the investor wants to assess the sentiment surrounding XYZ Coin to gauge the potential market response and overall sentiment towards the cryptocurrency.

The investor starts by utilizing sentiment analysis techniques to analyse social media platforms, online forums, and news articles related to XYZ Coin. They use sentiment lexicons and machine learning algorithms to gather insights into the sentiment of investors and the public.

Through sentiment lexicons, the investor identifies positive sentiment keywords such as "innovative," "game-changing," and "promising" associated with XYZ Coin. These positive sentiment scores indicate a generally favourable sentiment towards the cryptocurrency.

Additionally, the investor trains a machine learning algorithm using a labelled dataset of social media posts and news articles about XYZ Coin. The algorithm learns to classify sentiments as positive, negative, or neutral based on the labelled data. The investor feeds new social media posts and news articles into the trained algorithm to classify their sentiment.

By monitoring social media platforms, online forums, and news articles, the investor observes a surge in positive sentiment towards XYZ Coin following a major partnership announcement. This real-time sentiment analysis enables the investor to identify the positive market reaction and anticipate potential price movements.

Based on the sentiment analysis results, the investor decides to invest in XYZ Coin, considering the overall positive sentiment and the potential for growth. The sentiment analysis provides valuable insights that inform the investor's decision-making process and helps mitigate potential risks associated with investing in cryptocurrencies.

In summary, sentiment analysis in crypto investing enables investors to gain a comprehensive understanding of the sentiment surrounding a particular cryptocurrency. By leveraging sentiment lexicons, machine learning algorithms, and real-time monitoring of social media platforms, online forums, and news articles, investors can make more informed decisions about their crypto investments. Sentiment analysis provides actionable insights into market sentiment, helping investors identify trends, anticipate market reactions, and adjust their investment strategies accordingly.

2.9 Market Indicators

Market indicators are tools used by investors and traders to gain insights into the overall market conditions and make informed decisions. These indicators provide valuable information about the current and future trends in the market. In the context of cryptocurrency investing, market indicators can help investors analyse historical data, identify patterns, and understand potential market cycles.

Market indicators can be broadly categorized into two types: technical indicators and fundamental indicators. Technical indicators are based on price and volume data, while fundamental indicators consider factors such as market dominance, trading volume, and market breadth.

2.9.1 Familiarize yourself with key market indicators

1. Trading Volume: Trading volume refers to the number of shares or contracts traded in a particular cryptocurrency over a given period. High trading volume indicates active participation in the market and can be a sign of increasing interest or liquidity. Low trading volume, on the other hand, may suggest a lack of interest or limited liquidity.

Example: Suppose the trading volume of a cryptocurrency has been consistently increasing over the past week. This indicates a growing interest and participation in the market, which could potentially lead to price movements.

2. Market Dominance: Market dominance refers to the percentage share of a particular cryptocurrency's market capitalization compared to the total market capitalization of all cryptocurrencies. It provides insights into the relative strength and popularity of a specific cryptocurrency within the market.

Example: If a cryptocurrency has a high market dominance, it means that it holds a significant portion of the total market capitalization. This indicates that the cryptocurrency is widely adopted and has a strong presence in the market.

3. Market Breadth: Market breadth measures the number of cryptocurrencies participating in a particular market trend. It helps investors determine the overall strength and direction of the market.

Example: If many cryptocurrencies are experiencing positive price movements, it suggests that the market trend is bullish and there is broad-based participation. Conversely, if only a few cryptocurrencies are performing well while others are lagging, it may indicate a weak market trend.

By familiarizing yourself with these key market indicators, you can gain insights into the overall market conditions and make more informed investment decisions.

2.9.2 Analyse historical data and trends

Analysing historical data and trends is an essential part of understanding market cycles and identifying patterns in the cryptocurrency market. By studying past price movements and market behaviour, investors can gain valuable insights into potential future trends.

Example: Let's say you are analysing the historical data of a particular cryptocurrency and notice a recurring pattern where the price tends to increase after a period of consolidation. This pattern suggests that there might be a potential market cycle where the cryptocurrency consolidates for a period before experiencing a price surge.

Identifying these patterns and market cycles can help investors time their entry and exit points more effectively, maximizing their potential returns.

Also, technical analysis tools and indicators are available to
investors for further elucidation of past data and trends. These tools include moving averages, trend lines, support and resistance levels, and oscillators like the Relative Strength Index (RSI) or Moving Average Convergence Divergence (MACD). These indicators can provide insights into price momentum, trend strength, and potential reversal points.

By combining the analysis of historical data, patterns, and technical indicators, investors can develop a more comprehensive understanding of the cryptocurrency market and make more informed investment decisions.

Market indicators are essential for understanding market conditions, trends, and potential cycles in crypto investing. By familiarizing yourself with key indicators such as trading volume, market dominance, and market breadth, and analysing historical data and trends, you can gain a better understanding of the market and make informed investment decisions.

2.10 Fundamental Trends

In addition to technical indicators, fundamental analysis is an important aspect of crypto investing. Fundamental trends refer to the underlying factors that can impact the value and growth potential of cryptocurrencies. These factors help investors understand the long-term viability and intrinsic value of a cryptocurrency. Let's explore some key fundamental trends and their significance in crypto investing.

1. Adoption and Use Case:

The adoption and use case of a cryptocurrency can have a significant impact on its value. Investors should analyse whether a cryptocurrency has real applications and whether it is accepted by companies and individuals. The more a cryptocurrency is used, the greater its growth potential.

Example: Ethereum (ETH) is a cryptocurrency that has gained significant popularity due to its smart contract functionality. Many decentralized applications (dApps) and blockchain projects are based on the Ethereum platform, which has contributed to its value and market demand.

2. Development Team and Community:

The development team behind a cryptocurrency plays an important role in its success. Investors should evaluate the experience, expertise and reputation of team members. Additionally, the size and engagement of a cryptocurrency community can indicate its popularity and potential for future growth.

Example: Cardano (ADA) is a cryptocurrency known for its strong development team and active community. This group includes well-known blockchain scientists and experts. This helped Cardano gain credibility and a loyal community of supporters.

3. Partnerships and Collaborations:

Partnerships and collaborations can positively impact the value and adoption of cryptocurrencies. Investors should pay attention to whether the cryptocurrency cooperates with reputable companies or organizations. Such partnerships can provide opportunities for integration and wider acceptance of the cryptocurrency.

Example: Ripple (XRP) has formed partnerships with various financial institutions and payment providers, allowing for faster and more cost-effective cross-border transactions. These partnerships have increased the utility and demand for Ripple's cryptocurrency.

4. Regulatory Environment:

The regulatory environment can significantly impact the cryptocurrency market. Investors should stay informed about regulatory changes and developments in different jurisdictions. Regulatory clarity and favourable regulations can foster investor confidence and drive market growth.

Example: In recent years, countries like Switzerland, Singapore, and Malta have established clear and favourable regulations for cryptocurrencies and blockchain technology. This has attracted crypto businesses and investors to these jurisdictions, leading to increased market activity.

5. Market Demand and User Adoption:

The overall market demand and user adoption of a cryptocurrency can determine its value and growth potential. Investors should analyse whether a cryptocurrency has a strong user base and if it is gaining traction among mainstream users.

Example: Bitcoin (BTC) is the most well-known and widely adopted cryptocurrency. Its large user base and acceptance by businesses and merchants have contributed to its market dominance and value.

6. Technological Advancements:

Technological advancements in the cryptocurrency industry can drive innovation and impact the value of cryptocurrencies. Investors should stay updated on the latest developments, such as scalability solutions, privacy enhancements, and interoperability protocols.

Example: The introduction of Layer 2 solutions like the Lightning Network has addressed Bitcoin's scalability issues, allowing for faster and cheaper transactions. Technological advancements like these can increase the utility and demand for cryptocurrencies.

By considering these fundamental trends, investors can gain insights into the long-term prospects and value proposition of cryptocurrencies. However, it is important to note that fundamental analysis is subjective and requires thorough research and analysis. It is recommended to combine fundamental analysis with other forms of analysis, such as technical analysis and market indicators, to make well-informed investment decisions.

2.10.1 Stay updated on the latest news and developments in the cryptocurrency industry

Staying updated on the latest news and developments in the cryptocurrency industry is crucial for crypto investors. The cryptocurrency market is dynamic and constantly evolving, and staying informed can help investors make informed decisions and stay ahead of market trends. Here are some reasons why it's important to keep up with the latest news and developments:

1. Market Insights: By staying abreast of the latest news, investors can gain valuable information about market trends, investors and emerging opportunities. News articles, market analysis and expert opinions can provide valuable information that can help investors make informed decisions.

2. Regulatory Changes: The cryptocurrency industry is subject to evolving regulations. Being aware of regulatory changes can help investors understand the legal and compliance landscape that may affect market dynamics and investment strategies. By staying informed, investors can adjust their investment decisions to comply with regulations and mitigate risks.

3. Technology Developments: The cryptocurrency industry is driven by technological advancements. Investors can identify projects with innovative technology and long-term growth potential by staying current with the latest developments in blockchain technology, such as new protocols for managing transactions on a large scale, s

calability solutions for project management, or privacy enhancements.

4. Project Updates: Many cryptocurrencies are backed by projects and teams that regularly provide updates on their progress and milestones. Staying updated on project updates can help investors assess the viability and progress of a project, which can impact the potential value of the associated cryptocurrency.

5. Market Sentiment: The cryptocurrency market is influenced by investor sentiment. News and developments can shape market sentiment, leading to fluctuations in prices and market dynamics. By staying updated, investors can gauge market sentiment and make decisions based on market trends.

6. Investment Strategies: Staying updated on the latest news and developments can help investors refine their investment strategies. By understanding market trends and developments, investors can adjust their portfolio allocation, identify potential investment opportunities, and manage risk effectively.

To stay updated on the cryptocurrency industry, investors can follow reputable news sources, subscribe to newsletters, and engage with the crypto community through forums and social media platforms. Additionally, attending conferences and webinars can provide valuable insights and networking opportunities.

Staying updated on the latest news and developments in the cryptocurrency industry is crucial for investors. It provides valuable insights into market trends, regulatory changes, technological advancements, and project updates. By staying informed, investors can make well-informed investment decisions and navigate the dynamic and evolving crypto market effectively.

2.10.2 Monitor macroeconomic factors, regulatory changes, and technological advancements that can influence the market

Successful crypto investing requires monitoring various factors that can influence the market. In addition to fundamental and technical analysis, it is important to consider macroeconomic factors, regulatory changes, and technological advancements. Let's explore the significance of monitoring these factors:

1. Macroeconomic Factors:
Macroeconomic factors, such as inflation rates, interest rates, and geopolitical events, can impact the overall market sentiment and investor behaviour. Cryptocurrencies, like other financial assets, are not immune to macroeconomic trends. Monitoring these factors can help investors anticipate market movements and adjust their investment strategies accordingly.

Example: During times of economic uncertainty, investors may seek alternative investments like cryptocurrencies as a hedge against traditional markets. Monitoring macroeconomic factors can help investors identify such opportunities.

2. Regulatory Changes:
The regulatory landscape for cryptocurrencies is constantly evolving. Governments and regulatory bodies worldwide are developing frameworks to govern cryptocurrencies and digital assets. Monitoring regulatory changes is crucial as they can impact market sentiment, investor confidence, and the legal environment for cryptocurrencies.

Example: Regulatory changes, such as the introduction of favourable regulations or bans on cryptocurrencies in certain jurisdictions, can have a significant impact on the market. Investors should stay updated on regulatory developments to assess the potential risks and opportunities associated with specific cryptocurrencies.

3. Technological Advancements:
Technological advancements in the cryptocurrency industry can drive innovation and impact the value of cryptocurrencies. Staying informed about the latest developments, such as new blockchain protocols, scalability solutions, or privacy enhancements, can help investors identify projects with innovative technology and

long-term growth potential.

Example: The introduction of new consensus algorithms or advancements in privacy solutions can make cryptocurrencies more secure and efficient, attracting more investors and users. Monitoring technological developments can help investors identify promising projects.

By monitoring macroeconomic factors, regulatory changes and
technological developments, investors can stay informed about market conditions and make informed investment decisions. It is recommended that you regularly follow reputable news sources, attend industry conferences, and interact with the crypto community to stay informed of these factors.

The cryptocurrency market is characterized by extreme volatility and rapid changes. Therefore, it is advisable to thoroughly research, consider various varia bles, and seek guidance from financial professionals before investing.

In this chapter, we have discussed the key steps involved in getting started with cryptocurrency investments.Through the creation of an electronic fund, sel ecting the appropriate cryptocurrency to invest in, and following market trends can improve investment decisions by leveraging their digital currency management skills. To achieve optimal results, it is essential to conduct extensive research, diversify investments, and remain knowledgeable about emerging market trends and developments. Adapting and improving investment plans is crucial in the constantly evolving cryptocurrency market.

Chapter 3: Fundamental Concepts of Crypto Investment

3.0 Introduction

In this chapter, we will delve into the fundamental concepts of crypto investment. The concepts we will cover in each section will be explained more fully, with supporting statistics and relevant information to back up our arguments.

3.1 Blockchain Technology Explained

Blockchain technology is the underlying technology behind cryptocurrencies. A distributed and decentralized ledger is used to record transactions between multiple computers or nodes. In this section, we will provide a detailed explanation of blockchain technology and its key features.

Blockchain technology operates on the principles of transparency, immutability, and decentralization. It enables secure and transparent transactions without the need for intermediaries such as banks. Each transaction is recorded in a block and then added to the blockchain, creating 'time-stamped' transactions.

One of the main advantages of blockchain technology is its immutability. A transaction's record on the blockchain guarantees its integrity by preventing any manipulation or modification. This ensures data security. This makes blockchain technology extremely secure and fraud-proof.

Another important aspect of blockchain technology is its decentralization. Traditional financial systems rely on centralized authorities to validate and settle transactions. Conversely, the use of blockchain technology enables the management and control over transactions through a network of participants known as nodes. Decentralization eliminates the need for a central authority, making the system more resilient and less susceptible to censorship.

To illustrate the power of blockchain technology, let's consider the example of supply chain management. Traditional systems make it difficult to track the movement of goods, resulting in time-consuming and complicated processes. However, with blockchain technology, every step of the supply chain can be recorded on the blockchain, providing transparency and traceability. This enhances trust and reduces the risk of counterfeit goods entering the market.

3.2 Cryptocurrency Mining and Proof-of-Stake

Cryptocurrency mining is the process of validating and adding transactions to the blockchain. The use of computational power to solve intricate mathematical problems is necessary for veri fying and securing transactions. Throughout this section, we will discuss cryptocurrency mining and the concept of proof-of-stake.

During the initial stages of coin to bitcoin and other digital currencies, mining was mainly carried out on high-powered computers and specific hardware. Miners engaged in mathematical co mpetitions, and the first person to solve a puzzle would receive newly minted coins. This process ensured the security and integrity of the blockchain.

However, mining cryptocurrencies like Bitcoin has become increasingly resource-intensive and energy-consuming. This has led to the emergence of alternative consensus mechanisms, such as proof-of-stake (PoS). PoS is a consensus algorithm that involves selecting validators to generate new blocks according to the number of coins they hold and their willingness to take risks as collateral.

In a proof-of-stake system, validators are selected to create new blocks based on their stake in the network. The more coins a validator has and is willing to stake, the greater the probability of being selected to form. A new block was then created. Energy-intensive mining is less necessary, resulting in increased energy efficiency of the network.

Let's take Ethereum as an illustration of how proof-of-stake works. In the Ethereum network, validators can stake their Ether (the native cryptocurrency of Ethereum) to participate in the consensus process. Validators are chosen to create new blocks based on their stake, and they are rewarded with transaction fees.

Proof-of-stake has gained popularity due to its energy efficiency and lower resource requirements compared to traditional mining. It also reduces the risk of centralization, as validators are chosen based on their stake, rather than computational power. This makes the network more decentralized and secure.

3.3 Security and Wallet Management

Security is of utmost importance when it comes to crypto investment. This section provides information on the best practices and security measures for managing cryptocurrency wallets.

Cryptocurrency wallets are virtual storage devices that hold your private keys and enable you to access and operate your cryptocurrency assets. It is crucial to secure your wallets to prevent unauthorized access and potential loss of funds.

One of the fundamental security measures is to use a strong and unique password for your wallet. Avoid using common passwords or easily guessable information. Utilize uppercase and lowercase letters, numerical values, and special characters to generate a strong password.

Another important aspect of wallet security is two-factor authentication (2FA). 2FA adds an extra layer of security by requiring an additional verification step, such as a code sent to your mobile device, when accessing your wallet. Even if someone has access to your password, they will still need the second authentication factor to access that fund.

Additionally, it is crucial to keep your wallet software up to date. Wallet providers regularly release updates that include security patches and bug fixes. Staying up to date with these updates helps protect against potential vulnerabilities and ensures the security of your assets.

The choice of a wallet can be made in various ways, including hardware wallets, software wallet options, and online ones. Hardware wallets, such as Ledger and Trezor, provide an extra layer of security by storing your private keys offline. Software wallets, on the other hand, are applications that run on your computer or mobile device. Online wallets are web-based wallets that store your private keys on a remote server.

Each type of wallet has its advantages and considerations. Hardware wallets are considered the most secure option as they keep your private keys offline, protecting them from online threats. While software wallets are convenient and easy to use, they are more susceptible to malware attacks and hacking attempts. Online wallets offer convenience but come with the risk of third-party breaches.

It is also essential to be aware of phishing attempts and scams targeting cryptocurrency users. Beware of suspicious emails, websites or messages that ask for your wallets or private keys. Always verify the authenticity of the source before disclosing sensitive information.

The key to achieving success in cryptocurrency investing is familiarity with the fundamentals of blockchain technology, cryptocurrency mining, and wallet security. Blockchain technology provides transparency, immutability and decentralization and revolutionizes various industries. Cryptocurrency mining ensures the security and integrity of blockchain networks, while Proof-of-Stake offers an energy-efficient alternative. Proper wallet management and security measures protect your funds from unauthorized access and potential loss. Using these basic concepts and best practices, you can confidently navigate the world of crypto investing.

In this chapter, we covered the basic concepts of crypto investing. Related investments. We have provided detailed explanations of blockchain technology, cryptocurrency mining and wallet security. Understanding these concepts is critical to successful crypto investing.

In Section 1, we explained blockchain technology, which is the underlying technology behind cryptocurrencies. Blockchain is built on the principles of transparency, immutability, and decentralizations. It enables secure and transparent transactions without the need for intermediaries. By ensuring transparency and traceability, blockchain technology could transform industries like supply chain management.

Section 2 focused on cryptocurrency mining and introduced the concept of proof-of-stake. Mining in cryptocurrencies involves verifying and subsequently adding transactions to the blockchain. The development of proof-of-stake and other consensus mechanisms has been prompted by the growing demand for resources in mining. Proof-of-stake is a more energy-efficient and decentralized approach to creating new blocks in the blockchain.

In Section 3, we discussed the importance of wallet security and provided best practices for managing cryptocurrency wallets. Maintaining strong and unique passwords, implementing two-factor authentication, and updating wallet software are all vital factors. The choice between a hardware, software, or online wallet is determined by both personal preferences and security measures. How can one choose the best option? It' s also important to be aware of phishing and scam attempts targeting cryptocurrency users.

Understanding these basic concepts and following best practices will help you navigate the world of crypto investing with confidence.
To enhance your comprehension and up-to-date knowledge of the latest happenings in the crypto realm, it is essential to conduct additional research and analysis.

Chapter 4: Strategies for Successful Crypto Investments

4.0 Introduction

In this chapter, we will explore strategies that can help you make informed and successful crypto investments. We will provide more in-depth explanations, examples, and relevant statistics and data to support each strategy. The following methods can help you achieve positive returns in the crypto market.

4.1 Long-Term vs. Short-Term Investing

When it comes to crypto investments, one of the first decisions you need to make is whether you want to adopt a long-term or short-term investment approach. Each approach has its advantages and considerations.

Long-term investing involves holding onto your crypto assets for an extended period, usually years. The strategy is based on the idea that cryptocurrencies will maintain their value and increase in value over time. Long-term investors often focus on fundamental analysis, evaluating the project's technology, team, and potential use cases.

Take Bitcoin, for example. In 2010, the price of one Bitcoin was less than one dollar. However, long-term investors who held their Bitcoin saw its value rise to more than $60,000 in 2021. By taking a long-term investment approach, they have been able to enjoy significant price increases.

On the other hand, short-term investments are all about buying and selling crypto assets in relatively short periods of time, often days or weeks. Short-term traders are individuals who aim to capitalize on short-run price fluctuations. They rely on technical analysis, studying charts and patterns to predict short-term price movements.

A short-term investor could capitalize on a series of price fluctuations in cryptocurrencies to earn quick profits. However, short-term investing can be more volatile and requires active monitoring of the market.

It is essential to consider your investment goals, risk tolerance, and time commitment when deciding between long-term and short-term investing. Certain investors opt to use a mix of strategies, devoting primarily XYZ investments to long-term stocks and actively participating in trading with another portion of their portfolio.

4.2 Dollar-Cost Averaging and Portfolio Diversification

Dollar-cost averaging (DCA) and portfolio diversification are two strategies that can help mitigate risks and potentially enhance returns in crypto investments.

DCA is a strategy where you invest a fixed amount of money at regular intervals, regardless of the asset's price. The principle of buying more at a lower price and buying less at an elevated price is realized through consistent investment over time. DCA helps smooth out the impact of market volatility and reduces the risk of making poor investment decisions based on short-term price movements.

For example, suppose you decide to invest $100 in Bitcoin every month for a year. A high Bitcoin price will lead to a decrease in your overall Bitcoin purchase, while reducing it will result in an increase. Over time, this strategy can help you accumulate more assets at an average cost, regardless of short-term price fluctuations.

Portfolio diversification is another essential strategy in crypto investments. It involves spreading your investment across different cryptocurrencies and other asset classes. The key to avoiding being heavily invested in a single cryptocurrency or market segment is to have diversified assets in your portfolio.

To illustrate, instead of putting all your money into one cryptocurrency like Bitcoin, you can put some in other cryptocurrencies such as Ethereum, Ripple or Litecoin. Additionally, you can consider diversifying into other investment vehicles like decentralized finance (DeFi) tokens, non-fungible tokens (NFTs), or even traditional assets like stocks and bonds.

Diversification helps protect your portfolio from the volatility and potential risks associated with individual cryptocurrencies. It permits you to benefit from the expansion of multiple assets and minimizes the impact of sudden price fluctuations in a specific asset. By spreading your investments across different cryptocurrencies and asset classes, you can potentially achieve a more stable and balanced portfolio.

4.3 Identifying Promising Projects and ICOs

Identifying promising projects and initial coin offerings (ICOs) is another crucial strategy for successful crypto investments. ICOs are fundraising events in which new cryptocurrencies or tokens are offered to investors in exchange for established cryptocurrencies like Bitcoin or Ethereum.

When evaluating ICOs and projects, it is essential to conduct thorough research and due diligence. Here are some factors to consider:

1. Team and background: Assess the experience, expertise and experience of the project team. Look for teams with strong expertise in the field and a track record of successful projects.

2. Technology and innovation: Assessing the technology and innovation behind the project. Does it offer a unique solution or improvement to an existing problem? Is there a clear use case for the proposed cryptocurrency or token?

3. Market Potential: Consider the market potential and demand for the project's product or service. Is there a target market for the project and does it have the potential for widespread adoption?

4. Community and Partnerships: Check the community relationship and partnership of the project. A strong and active community can be an indicator of a project's popularity and growth potential. Partnerships with established companies or organizations can also lend credibility to the project.

5. Whitepaper and Roadmap: Read the project's whitepaper and roadmap to understand the project's goals,

timeline, and implementation plan. Look for a well-defined roadmap and a clear vision for the project's future.

6. Tokenomics and Distribution: Analyse the tokenomics of the project, including the token supply, distribution, and token utility. Understanding how the tokens will be used within the project's ecosystem can provide insights into the potential value and demand for the token.

It is crucial to note that investing in ICOs and early-stage projects carries higher risks compared to established cryptocurrencies. Therefore, thorough research and due diligence are essential to mitigate risks and make informed investment decisions.

The implementation of these techniques can enhance your crypto investment strategy, allowing you to thrive in the constantly evolving and unpredictable crypto market. It is important to adapt and adjust your strategies based on market conditions, stay current with industry developments, and keep up with crypto-focused education.

4.4 Risk Management and Security Measures in Crypto Investments

Effective risk management is crucial to minimize potential losses and protect your capital. Here are some risk management strategies to consider:

1. Set Clear Investment Goals: Define your investment goals and determine the level of risk you are willing to take. This will help you make informed decisions and avoid impulsive trading based on short-term market fluctuations.

2. Diversify Your Portfolio: As mentioned earlier, diversifying your portfolio is an essential risk management technique. By spreading your investments across cryptocurrencies and asset classes, you can reduce the exposure to volatility in a single asset.

3. Ensure Adequate Risk Capital: Only invest funds that you can afford to lose. Crypto investing can be very volatile, and it is important to allocate capital that you are comfortable with in the event of a market downturn.

4. Stay informed: Stay up to date with the latest news, market trends and regulatory developments in the crypto space. Good information can help you make better decisions and predict potential risks.

5. Use Stop Orders: Consider using stop-loss orders to limit potential losses. A stop loss order will automatically sell your cryptocurrency when it reaches the present price, helping you minimize losses if the market moves against you.

6. Monitor Your Investments Regularly: Monitor your investments regularly and review your portfolio regularly. This allows you to identify potential risks or opportunities in time and make the necessary adjustments.

4.5 Security Measures

Ensuring the security of your crypto investments is important. Here are some safety measures to implement:

1. Use Strong Passwords: Create strong and unique passwords for your crypto exchange accounts and wallets. Avoid using easy-to-guess passwords and consider using a password manager to keep your login information secure.

2. Enable Two-Factor Authentication (2FA): Enable 2FA for your crypto exchange accounts and wallets. 2FA provides an additional layer of security by requiring a second verification step in addition to your password, such as: B. a code sent to your mobile phone.

3. Choose reliable exchanges and wallets: Choose reliable and safe crypto exchanges and wallets. Read about their security features, data logging, and user reviews before trusting them with your money.

4. Update your software and hardware: Update your crypto wallets and software regularly to ensure you have

the latest security patches and features. Older software may contain vulnerabilities that can be exploited by hackers.

5. Beware of Phishing Attempts: Beware of phishing attempts where scammers pose as legitimate websites or sharing platforms to steal your login information. Always check the website URL and beware of spam emails or messages asking for personal information.

6. Secure Your Private Keys: Safely store your private keys, which are required to access your crypto assets. Offline paper wallets or hardware wallet options can be used to safeguard your private keys from online attacks. Why? (See below)

Through the implementation of these risk management methods, along with security measures, you can ensure that your crypto investments are protected from fraudulent activities or potential security breaches.

Risk management and security measures are essential components of successful crypto investments. The key to succeeding in the crypto market is to have clear investment objectives, maintain a diverse portfolio of investments
and ensure that you are not overlooking any potential risks.

In essence, successful crypto investment requires a combination of prudent strategies, research, and strategic thinking. By considering long-term investment to achieve greater confidence in the crypto market, you must balance your investment objectives by implementing dollar-cost averaging, portfolio diversification, and identifying projects and promising ICOs.

Chapter 5: Tools and Resources for Crypto Investors

5.0 Introduction

In this chapter, we will explore various tools and resources that can aid crypto investors in their decision-making process. These tools and resources provide valuable insights, analysis, and information about the cryptocurrency market, helping investors stay informed and make informed investment decisions. The market knowledge, potential investments, and crypto portfolio management capabilities are enhanced by these tools and resources for investors.

5.1 Crypto Exchanges and Trading Platforms

Crypto exchanges and trading platforms are essential tools for investors to buy, sell, and trade cryptocurrencies. These platforms offer a secure and hassle-free way to access the cryptocurrency market and engage in trades. Here are some popular crypto exchanges and trading platforms:

1. Binance: Binance is one of the largest and most popular crypto exchanges globally. It offers a wide range of cryptocurrencies for trading and offers advanced trading features such as margin trading and futures contracts.

2. Coinbase: Coinbase is a user-friendly cryptocurrency exchange that is widely used by both beginners and experienced investors. It supports various cryptocurrencies and provides a simple interface for buying and selling digital assets.

3. Kraken: Kraken is a reputable crypto exchange known for its robust security measures and comprehensive cryptocurrency. It offers advanced trading features and supports deposits and withdrawals in fiat currency.

4. eToro: eToro is a social trading platform that allows users to trade cryptocurrencies, stocks, and other assets. It offers a unique feature called "Copy Trading," where users can automatically copy the trades of successful traders.

5. Bitstamp: Bitstamp is one of the oldest crypto exchanges and is known for its focus on security and compliance. It provides a user-friendly interface and supports fiat currency deposits and withdrawals.

These exchanges and trading platforms are just a few

examples of the many crypto-related entities available in the market. It is essential for investors to research and choose a platform that suits their needs in terms of security, fees, supported cryptocurrencies, and trading features.

5.2 Cryptocurrency News and Analysis Websites

Staying updated with the latest news and analysis is crucial for crypto investors. Investing can benefit from the information, market trends and expert perspectives provided by both cryptocurrency and analytics websites. Here are some popular sites in this category:

1. CoinMarketCap: CoinMarketCap is a widely used platform for tracking cryptocurrency prices, market cap, volume and other market data. It provides real-time data for thousands of cryptocurrencies and offers various tools to analyse market trends.

2. CoinDesk: CoinDesk is a leading cryptocurrency news platform covering the latest developments, trends and analysis in the field of cryptography. It also hosts events and conferences that bring industry experts and enthusiasts together.

3. CryptoSlate: CryptoSlate is a comprehensive

cryptocurrency information platform. It provides news, analysis and research on various cryptocurrencies, blockchain projects and industry events.

4. Cointelegraph: Cointelegraph is a popular cryptocurrency news website that covers a wide range of topics, including market analysis, blockchain technology, and regulatory developments. It also includes interviews with industry leaders and experts.

5. CryptoCompare: CryptoCompare is a platform that provides real-time and historical data on cryptocurrencies, exchanges, and mining. It offers tools for comparing and analysing different cryptocurrencies and exchange platforms.

These websites offer a wealth of information and resources for crypto investors. Investors can gain insight into market trends, regulatory changes, and investment opportunities by regularly monitoring the news and analysis provided by these platforms.

In addition to the tools and resources described earlier, there are many other tools available that
can help improve your experience when investing in crypto. Let's explore some of them:

5.3 Portfolio Management Platforms

Managing a crypto portfolio effectively is crucial for investors. The use of portfolio management platforms allows for the centralization of cryptocurrency investment operations. These platforms offer features such as portfolio tracking, performance analysis and asset allocation tools. Here are some popular portfolio management platforms:

1. Blockfolio: Blockfolio is a widely used portfolio management application that allows users to track their cryptocurrencies, view real-time prices, and receive portfolio updates. It supports various cryptocurrencies and provides detailed charts and graphs for analysis.

2. Delta: Delta is another popular portfolio management program that offers a user-friendly interface and extensive features. It allows users to track their holdings, view price alerts, and analyse portfolio performance. It also provides tax reporting tools for easier tax compliance.

3. CoinStats: CoinStats is a comprehensive portfolio management platform that supports multiple exchanges and wallets. It offers real-time price tracking, portfolio performance analysis, and tax reporting features. It also provides a mobile app for on-the-go portfolio management.

These portfolio management platforms help investors keep track of their investments, monitor their portfolio performance, and make informed decisions based on real-time data.

5.4 Tax Reporting Tools

Tax compliance is an important aspect of crypto investing. The tax laws govern certain cryptographic transactions, and it can be challenging to accurately calculate and report tax events. Tax reporting tools help simplify the process by automatically tracking transactions and generating tax reports. Here are some popular tax reporting tools:

1. CoinTracking: CoinTracking is a widely used tax reporting platform that supports over 10,000 cryptocurrencies and integrates with popular exchanges. It automatically calculates capital gains, provides tax reporting, and offers features such as FIFO, LIFO, and HIFO accounting methods.

2. CryptoTrader Tax: CryptoTrader Tax is a user-friendly tax reporting software that automates the process of calculating cryptocurrency taxes. It provides support for various accounting techniques, inte

grates with widely used exchanges, and generates tax reports that are easy to submit to the IRS.

3. ZenLedger: ZenLedger is a comprehensive cryptocurrency tax software that offers features like automated transaction imports, tax loss harvesting, and tax optimization strategies. It supports various accounting methods and provides detailed tax reports for individuals and tax professionals.

By using these tax reporting tools, investors can ensure accurate tax reporting and compliance with tax regulations, saving time and minimizing the risk of errors.

5.5 Technical Analysis Software

Technical analysis plays a significant role in crypto trading. It involves analysing historical price and volume data to identify patterns and trends, helping investors make informed trading decisions. Technical analysis software offers advanced charting tools, indicators and analysis functions. Here is some popular technical analysis software:

1. TradingView: TradingView is a widely used platform that offers advanced charting tools and a wide range of technical indicators. It allows users to analyse price movements, draw trend lines and create custom indicators. It also provides a social community where

traders can share ideas and strategies.

2. Coinigy: Coinigy is a cryptocurrency trading and portfolio management platform that includes advanced technical analysis tools. It offers real-time charts, custom indicators and prices. It also integrates with several exchanges to facilitate trading.

3. CryptoCompare: In addition to data and news offerings, CryptoCompare also offers several technical analysis tools. It offers interactive charts, indicators and pattern recognition features. It also allows users to compare different cryptocurrencies and analyse their performance.

By utilizing technical analysis software, investors can gain a deeper understanding of market trends, identify potential entry and exit points, and improve their trading strategies. These tools provide a wide range of features and indicators that help investors analyse price patterns, identify support and resistance levels, and make informed trading decisions.

In addition to portfolio management platforms, tax reporting tools, and technical analysis software, there are several other tools and resources that cater to specific needs of crypto investors. Let's explore some of them:

5.6 Crypto News Aggregators

Staying updated with the latest news and developments in the cryptocurrency industry is crucial for investors. Crypto news aggregators gather news articles from various sources and provide a centralized platform for users to access the latest information. The categorization of news based on various cryptocurrencies, exchanges, and subjects is common among these platforms, making it simpler for investors to locate relevant content. Popular new cryptocurrency aggregators include:

1. CoinDesk: CoinDesk is the leading cryptocurrency news platform providing comprehensive coverage of the latest cryptocurrency
industry news, analysis and insights. It covers a wide range of topics including market trends, regulatory developments and blockchain technology.

2. Cointelegraph: Cointelegraph is another prominent crypto news aggregator that offers a wide range of news articles, analysis, and opinion pieces. Market updates, industry trends and
technological developments are among the topics covered.

3. CryptoSlate: CryptoSlate is a platform that provides news, analysis, and research on cryptocurrencies and blockchain technology. It includes features like ICO listings, market data, and in-depth project profiles.

By using crypto news aggregators, investors can stay

informed about the latest developments in the crypto industry, which can help them make more informed investment decisions.

5.7 Social Trading Platforms

Social trading platforms allow investors to connect with and follow successful traders, enabling them to replicate their trades and investment strategies. Trading strategies are discussed, insights shared, and cooperation established through these platforms. Popular social trading platforms in the crypto space are:

1. eToro: eToro is a leading social trading platform that allows users to copy the trades of successful traders. The product boasts an easy-to-use interface, numerous trading instruments, and a social network where users can engage in discussions about trading strategies.

2. ZuluTrade: ZuluTrade is a social trading platform that allows users to follow and copy the trades of professional traders. It offers a wide range of trading instruments, customizable risk management tools, and a social community for traders to connect and collaborate.

3. NAGA: NAGA is a social trading platform that combines social networking and trading features. It allows users to follow and copy the trades of successful traders,

interact with other traders, and access a wide range of trading instruments.

By utilizing social trading platforms, investors can benefit from the expertise of successful traders and potentially improve their investment performance.

5.8 Security and Wallet Solutions

Security is a critical aspect of crypto investing. It is essential to store cryptocurrencies securely and protect them from potential threats. Wallet solutions provide a secure way to store and manage cryptocurrencies. Common wallet solutions include:

1. Hardware wallets: Hardware wallets are physical devices that store private keys offline and provide an additional layer of security. Examples of hardware wallets are Ledger Nano S, Trezor, and KeepKey.

2. Software Wallets: Software wallets are applications that can be installed on computers or mobile devices. They offer a convenient way to store and manage cryptocurrencies. Popular software wallets include Exodus, MyEtherWallet, and Atomic Wallet.

3. Online Wallets: Online wallets are web wallets that allow users to access their cryptocurrencies from anywhere

with an internet connection. Examples of online wallets are Coinbase Wallet, MetaMask, and Binance Wallet.

The use of secure wallets by investors can help them protect
their digital assets from potential theft or hacking. Hardware wallets like Ledger and Trezor store private keys offline and are considered one of the most secure ways to store cryptocurrencies. The management of cryptocurrencies on computers or mobile devices is made easier by software wallets like Exodus and MyEtherWallet. Online wallets, such as Coinbase Wallet and MetaMask, offer the flexibility to access cryptocurrencies from any device with an internet connection.

It is important for investors to select wallet solutions that are compatible with their
security interests and requirements. By utilizing secure wallet solutions, investors can have peace of mind knowing that their cryptocurrencies are protected.

5.9 Education and Learning Resources

The cryptocurrency market is constantly evolving, and staying informed about the latest trends, technologies, and investment strategies is essential for investors. Investors can gain valuable insights from a range of educational materials covering the crypto space. Some popular educational resources include:

1. Online Courses: Online platforms like Udemy and Coursera offer a wide range of courses on cryptocurrency and blockchain technology. These courses cover topics such as cryptocurrency trading, blockchain basics, and smart contract development.

2. Blogs and Newsletters: Many cryptographic experts share their insights and analysis in blogs and newsletters. Popular crypto blogs include CoinCentral, Crypto Briefing, and The Block. By subscribing to these blogs and newsletters, investors can gain valuable information and perspectives.

3. YouTube Channels and Podcasts: There are several YouTube channels and podcasts dedicated to discussing cryptocurrencies and blockchain technology. Ivan on Tech, Coin Bureau and
Crypto Tips are some of the popular channels. These channels and podcasts often feature interviews with industry experts and provide educational content for investors.

By utilizing educational resources, investors can stay updated with the latest developments in the crypto space, understand different investment strategies, and make informed decisions.

In summary, there exist various tools and materials designed to make investing in crypto a more enjoyable experience. Technical analysis software, educational materials, and other tools are available to investors, providing them with information on the crypto industry, portfolio management, tax reporting, or technical analysis. These tools and resources provide investors with the ability to navigate the crypto market more efficiently and make informed investment choices.

Chapter 6: Overcoming Challenges in Crypto Investing

6.0 Introduction

In this chapter, we will explore the various challenges that crypto investors face and discuss strategies to overcome them. We will provide in-depth explanations, relevant statistics, and case studies to support our points.

Having an understanding and acting on these challenges will enable investors to invest in the crypto space with confidence.

6.1 Dealing with Volatility and Market Corrections

One of the key challenges in crypto investing is the high level of volatility in the market. Market sentiment, regulatory changes, and technological advancements are among the many factors that contribute to the volatility of cryptocurrencies. To successfully navigate this volatility, investors need to understand the underlying factors and develop strategies to mitigate the risks.

Examples:

1. Diversification: Diversifying your crypto portfolio is a common strategy to reduce the impact of market volatility. By investing in a variety of cryptocurrencies across different sectors, you can spread the risk and potentially offset losses in one asset with gains in another.

2. Dollar-cost averaging: This strategy involves investing a fixed amount of money at regular intervals, regardless of the cryptocurrency's price. The long-term nature of cryptocurrencies can be exploited by investors through the consistent buying of these monies, rather than experiencing short-

and medium-chain price fluctuations.

3. Setting stop-loss orders: Stop-loss orders allow investors to set a predetermined price at which their cryptocurrency holdings will be automatically sold. This protects against large losses in the event of a market correction or a sudden price drop.

6.2 Avoiding Fraud and Fraudulent Projects

The crypto market is also affected by fraud and fraudulent projects. It is important for investors to exercise caution and do thorough research before investing in any cryptocurrency project. Investors should be alert and aware of the warning signs to prevent falling prey.

Examples:
1. Research the team: Before investing in a project, it is important to research the team behind it. Pay attention to their experience, professional experience and reliability. Beware of projects with unknown or inexperienced teams as they are more likely to engage in fraudulent activity.

2. Conduct in-depth analysis: evaluate the project's white paper, website, and community engagement. Make sure you have transparency, a roadmap and a strong community. Beware of projects that make

unrealistic claims or promise high profits without providing solid evidence.

3. Check regulatory compliance: Make sure the project complies with relevant regulations and has the necessary licenses and permits. Investing in projects that operate outside the legal framework can expose investors to legal risks and potential loss of funds.

6.3 Taxation and Legal Considerations

Crypto investments can have tax implications, and it is crucial for investors to understand the tax laws and regulations in their respective jurisdictions. Failing to comply with tax obligations can result in penalties and legal consequences. Investors should also be aware of the legal aspects of crypto investing, including regulatory changes and potential limitations.

Examples:
1. Consult a tax professional: Seek advice from a tax professional who specializes in cryptocurrency taxation. Their expertise extends to advising on reporting requirements, tax deductions, and ways to lower tax expenses.

2. Keep detailed records: Maintain accurate records of all cryptocurrency transactions, including purchases, sales, and transfers. This will help in calculating capital gains or

losses and ensure compliance with tax regulations.

3. Stay updated with regulatory changes: Stay informed about regulatory developments in the crypto space. Governments around the world are continually updating their regulations, and investors should be aware of any changes that may impact their investments.

In this chapter, we explore the obstacles that crypto investors encounter and offer solutions to overcome them. By understanding and implementing these strategies, investors can navigate the crypto market with confidence and make informed investment decisions. Managing volatility and market corrections requires proactive steps such as diversification of the portfolio, use of dollar-cost averaging, and setting stop-loss orders. These strategies help mitigate the impact of short-term price fluctuations and protect against significant losses.

When it comes to avoiding scams and fraudulent projects, thorough research and due diligence are crucial. The team responsible for a project should be scrutinized by investors, considering their experience and credibility. Evaluating the project's whitepaper, website, and community engagement is also important to identify any red flags or unrealistic claims. Additionally, ensuring regulatory compliance and legal considerations is essential to protect investments and avoid potential legal risks.

Taxation and legal considerations are important aspects of crypto investing. Getting in touch with a tax professional who has expertise in handling cryptocurrency taxes can offer valuable insights into the reporting process, tax deductions, and tax planning techniques. Keeping detailed records of all cryptocurrency transactions is necessary for accurate tax reporting. It is also important to stay updated with regulatory changes as governments continue to update their regulations in the crypto space.

Ultimately, investors can overcome challenges in crypto investing by comprehending and resolving the issues presented in this chapter. Implementing strategies to deal with volatility, avoiding scams and fraudulent projects, and considering taxation and legal aspects will help investors navigate the crypto market successfully. It is important to stay informed, conduct thorough research, and seek professional advice when needed to make informed investment decisions. Investing in the crypto market requires frequent updates on the latest happenings. Keeping up with news, market analysis, and industry insights can provide valuable information that can guide investment decisions. Subscribing to reputable cryptocurrency publications, following influential figures in the industry, and participating in online communities can help investors stay updated and gain valuable insights.

Investors should also keep an eye on their emotions

and refrain from making impulsive investment decisions based on short-term market fluctuations. The crypto market can be highly volatile, and it is common for prices to experience significant fluctuations in a short period. The key to investing is to avoid fear or FOMO and instead focus on researching and analyzing the long-term ahead. This approach should be taken with caution.

Lastly, investors should consider the security of their crypto assets. The decentralized nature of cryptocurrencies means that individuals are responsible for safeguarding their own funds. Utilizing secure wallets, implementing strong passwords, enabling two-factor authentication, and being cautious of phishing attempts are some of the measures that can help protect against hacks and theft.

The adoption of these strategies can assist investors in overcoming obstacles in the realm of crypto investing and propel them towards success. It is important to approach crypto investing with a long-term mindset, conduct thorough research, and seek professional advice when needed. With proper knowledge and cautious decision-making, investors can navigate the crypto market with confidence and potentially achieve their investment goals.

Chapter 7: Real-Life Examples and Case Studies

7.0 Introduction

In this chapter, we will delve into real-life examples and case studies to provide a deeper understanding of the concepts discussed throughout the book. These instances offer valuable insights into the triumphs and tragedies of those who invest in crypto, providing valuable lessons for our own investments.

7.1 Success Stories of Crypto Investors

Crypto investing has made headlines with numerous success stories of individuals who have achieved significant returns on their investments. While these success stories provide compelling evidence of the potential for significant returns in the crypto market, they also highlight the need for careful investment decisions and effective use of capital.

Crypto investing has witnessed remarkable success stories where individuals have achieved exceptional returns on their investments. These success stories serve as

inspiration for potential investors, showcasing the immense potential for wealth creation in the crypto market. Nonetheless, it
is crucial to comprehend the origins of these triumph stories and how they can be utilized in our own investment decisions.

Identifying and taking calculated risks in the early stages of their investments is one of the reasons why crypto
investors have been so successful. Erik Finman's story exemplifies this approach. At the age of 12, Finman invested $1,000 in Bitcoin when it was still in its infancy. His decision to invest early and hold onto his investment for the long term paid off generously, with his Bitcoin holdings reaching a value of over $4 million by the time he turned 18. This success story highlights the potential rewards of recognizing the potential of emerging technologies and having the patience to let investments grow.

Among the Winklevosses who achieved success were the twins who took Bitcoin as an early stage in their legal battle against Zuckerberg, adding another story about innovation and marketing. After receiving a $65 million settlement, they invested a significant portion of their funds into Bitcoin. Today, their Bitcoin holdings are estimated to be worth billions of dollars. The Winklevoss twins' success demonstrates the importance of capitalizing on opportunities presented by new technologies and having the financial means to invest in them.

It is important to note that these success stories are exceptional cases and should not be seen as the norm. The crypto market is highly volatile, and success on such a scale requires a unique set of circumstances, including early adoption, risk tolerance, and long-term commitment. However, these stories do provide valuable lessons that can be applied to our own investment strategies.

We must learn from these success stories that it is crucial to conduct extensive research
and critically evaluate them. Successful investors spend considerable time acquiring knowledge about the technology, the team behind the project, and the market dynamics. By understanding the fundamentals of a project and its potential for growth, investors can make more informed decisions and position themselves for success.

Also, successful
crypto investors make a point of diversifying their portfolios. They understand the risks associated with investing in a single asset and spread their investments across a variety of cryptocurrencies. It helps reduce the risk of large losses by allowing markets to adjust in response to fluctuations.

To support our analysis, let's look at some relevant statistics. According to the latest data, the crypto market's overall value was determined by the market cap. This remarkable figure showcases the growth and potential of the market. Additionally, the number of unique Bitcoin addresses has been steadily increasing, indicating a growing user base and adoption of cryptocurrencies.

Success stories of crypto investors highlight the potential for significant gains in the crypto market. While these stories are exceptional, they provide valuable lessons that can guide our own investment strategies. The combination of conducting extensive research, focusing on diversification, and adopting a long-term perspective is essential for us to succeed in the crypto space. The fact remains that investing in cryptocurrencies involves risks, and it is crucial to conduct thorough analysis and manage risk appropriately to navigate this dynamic market.

One notable success story is that of Erik Finman, who invested $1,000 in Bitcoin when he was just 12 years old. His investment grew exponentially over the years, and by the time he turned 18, his Bitcoin holdings were valued at over $4 million. Finman's story showcases the transformative power of early investments in cryptocurrencies and the potential for life-changing returns.

Another success story is that of the Winklevoss twins, Cameron and Tyler, who famously sued Mark Zuckerberg over the creation of Facebook. After receiving a settlement of $65 million, the twins invested a portion of their funds into Bitcoin, becoming early adopters of the cryptocurrency. Today, their Bitcoin holdings are estimated to be worth billions of dollars, solidifying their status as prominent figures in the crypto industry.

These success stories highlight the importance of strategic decision-making and a long-term investment approach. In both cases, the individuals recognized the potential of cryptocurrencies early on and made significant investments that paid off handsomely. However, it is important to note that these success stories are not representative of the average investor's experience and should not be viewed as guarantees of success.

7.2 Lessons Learned from Failed Investments

While success stories are inspiring, it is equally important to learn from the failures and mistakes of others. Failed investments can provide valuable lessons that help investors avoid common pitfalls and make more informed decisions.

One prominent example of a failed investment is the case of BitConnect. BitConnect was a cryptocurrency lending and exchange platform that promised high returns through its lending program. However, in early 2018, the platform was exposed as a Ponzi scheme, leading to its collapse and significant losses for investors. The BitConnect case serves as a cautionary tale about the importance of conducting thorough research and due diligence before investing in any project.

Another notable example is the infamous Mt. Gox incident. Mt. Gox was once the largest Bitcoin exchange in the world, handling a significant portion of Bitcoin transactions. However, in 2014, the exchange suffered a massive security breach, resulting in the loss of hundreds of millions of dollars' worth of Bitcoin. This incident highlights the importance of security measures and the need for investors to carefully choose reputable and secure platforms for trading and storing their cryptocurrencies.

These examples of failed investments underscore the need for caution and careful consideration when investing in the crypto market.
Researching projects thoroughly, analyzing their fundamentals and risk-
taking before investing is also important. Additionally, implementing robust security measures and choosing reliable platforms can help mitigate the risk of losses due to security breaches or fraudulent activities.

Finally, the world of crypto investing can be truly understood by utilizing real-life examples and case studies. By examining both success stories and failures, we can learn important lessons and apply them to our own investment strategies. These triumphs showcase the possibility of substantial gains in the crypto realm, while these tragedies underscore the importance of thorough research, due diligence, and security measures. Investors can gain confidence in the crypto market by adopting the strategies and concepts presented in this book, which will help them navigate it confidently.

The motivation behind success stories lies in gaining knowledge from those who have faced similar challenges and mistakes. Failed investments can provide valuable insights into the risks and pitfalls of crypto investing, helping us avoid similar mistakes and make more informed decisions. In addition, effective security measures are crucial for safeguarding investments. This includes using secure wallets to store cryptocurrencies, enabling two-factor authentication, and choosing reputable and regulated exchanges for trading. By taking these precautions, investors can minimize the risk of falling victim to security breaches or fraudulent activities.

In summary, it is just as

important to learn from investment failures and the success stories of crypto markets. These failures provide valuable lessons that can help investors avoid common pitfalls and make informed decisions. To succeed in the crypto space, one must conduct thorough research, exercise caution and implement appropriate due diligence and security measures. By combining these insights with the strategies and concepts presented in this book, investors can increase their chances of success and reduce potential risks.

Chapter 8: Conclusion and Next Steps

8.0 Introduction

The prospect of diversifying one's investments through cryptocurrency investment portfolios is exciting
and may result in significant profits for investors.
This book covers fundamental crypto investing concepts, strategies, tools, and challenges as well as providing the necessary guidance.

In Chapter 1, we discussed the basics of cryptocurrency investing, including what cryptocurrency is, why it is worth investing in, and the benefits and risks involved. The key concepts to consider when making investment decisions are already established.

Chapter 2 focused on getting started with cryptocurrency investments.
Our discussion cantered on developing an online digital wallet, investing in the appropriate cryptocurrencies, and following market trends. All of this was covered. These steps are essential for laying the foundation of a successful investment journey.

In Chapter 3, we delved into the fundamental concepts of crypto investment. We explained blockchain technology, the backbone of cryptocurrencies, and its potential applications.
We also covered cryptocurrency mining, proof-of-stake mechanisms and the need to ensure security and manage wallets so you can safely invest.

Chapter 4 provided strategies for successful crypto investments. We compared long-term and short-term investing approaches and discussed the benefits of dollar-cost averaging and portfolio diversification. We also stressed the need to conduct extensive research in order to identify good projects and early coin offerings (ICOs)

In Chapter 5, we explored the tools and resources available

to crypto investors. Our conversation covered both crypto exchanges and trading platforms, as well the news sites that provide cryptocurrency analysis and news. We also highlighted the significance of tracking and analysing crypto market data to make informed investment decisions.

Chapter 6 addressed the challenges faced by crypto investors. We discussed how to navigate volatility and market corrections, as well as how to avoid scams and fraudulent projects. We also discussed the taxation and legal aspects of crypto investments.

In Chapter 7, we presented real-life examples and case studies of successful crypto investors. Our discussion cantered on lessons learned from unsuccessful investments, emphasizing the importance of taking stock in both successful and unsuccessful crypto transactions.

8.1 Recap of Key Points

I. Cryptocurrency investing offers diversification and potential financial growth.
II. Understanding the basics, such as cryptocurrency and its advantages and disadvantages, is essential.

III. Setting up a digital wallet and choosing the right cryptocurrencies are essential steps.
IV. Market trends and analysis help in making informed investment decisions.
V. Blockchain technology, mining, and security are fundamental concepts to grasp.
VI. Long-term and short-term investing strategies have their own merits.
VII. Dollar-cost averaging and portfolio diversification reduce risks.
VIII. Thorough research is necessary to identify promising projects and ICOs.
IX. Crypto exchanges, news websites, and market analysis tools are valuable resources.
X. Dealing with volatility, avoiding scams, and understanding taxation are challenges to overcome.
XI. Learning from successful investors and failed investments provides valuable insights.

8.2 Building a Long-Term Crypto Investment Plan

Building a long-term crypto investment plan is crucial for achieving sustainable growth and minimizing risks. Here are some key steps to consider:

- Define your investment goals: Determine what you want to achieve with your crypto investments,

whether it's long-term wealth accumulation or funding a specific financial goal.
- Assess your risk tolerance: Understand your risk tolerance and adjust your investment strategy accordingly.
  Diversifying the use of different cryptocurrencies is necessary to minimize volatility.
- Research and analyse: Continuously research and analyse the crypto market to identify promising projects with strong fundamentals and potential for growth.
- Create a diversified portfolio: Spread your investments across different cryptocurrencies to reduce the impact of market fluctuations.

In conclusion, cryptocurrency investing offers an exciting and potentially lucrative opportunity for individuals looking to diversify their investment portfolios. Throughout this book, we have covered the basic principles (the fundamentals) strategies ("the methods"), instruments and problems encountered in crypto investing.

Reference

1. Andrianto Y, Diputra Y. The effect of cryptocurrency on investment portfolio effectiveness. Journal of Finance and Accounting. 2017;5(6):229-238

2. Barnes P. Crypto currency and its susceptibility to speculative bubbles, manipulation, scams and fraud. Journal of Advanced Studies in Finance (JASF). 2018;9((18)):60-77

3. Elendner H. F5: Optimised crypto-currency investment strategies. White paper, 2018. Available from: https://f5crypto.com/wp-content/uploads/2023/06/F5_Crypto_Index_Whitepaper-1.pdf

4. Erdogan, S., Ahmed, M. Y., & Sarkodie, S. A. (2022). Analyzing asymmetric effects of cryptocurrency demand on environmental sustainability. Environmental Science and Pollution Research, 29(21), 31723–31733. https://doi.org/10.1007/s11356-021-17998-y

5. Petukhina A, Trimborn S, Härdle WK, Elendner H. Investing with Cryptocurrencies-evaluating their potential for portfolio allocation strategies. arXiv preprint arXiv:2009.04461. 9 Sep 2020

6. Spenkelink H. The Adoption Process of Cryptocurrencies-Identifying Factors That Influence the Adoption of Cryptocurrencies from a Multiple Stakeholder Perspective. Enschede, Netherlands: University of Twente; 2014;1:1-103

7. Twomey D, Mann A. Fraud and manipulation within cryptocurrency markets. Corruption and Fraud in Financial Markets: Malpractice, Misconduct and Manipulation. 2020:205-249

www.ingramcontent.com/pod-product-compliance
Lightning Source LLC
Chambersburg PA
CBHW052205220526
45471CB00004B/1816